ISBN-13: 978-1-4234-5482-3
ISBN-10: 1-4234-5482-0

Walt Disney Music Company
Wonderland Music Company, Inc.

DISTRIBUTED BY

7777 W. BLUEMOUND RD. P.O. BOX 13819 MILWAUKEE, WI 53213

contents

Hannah Montana 2

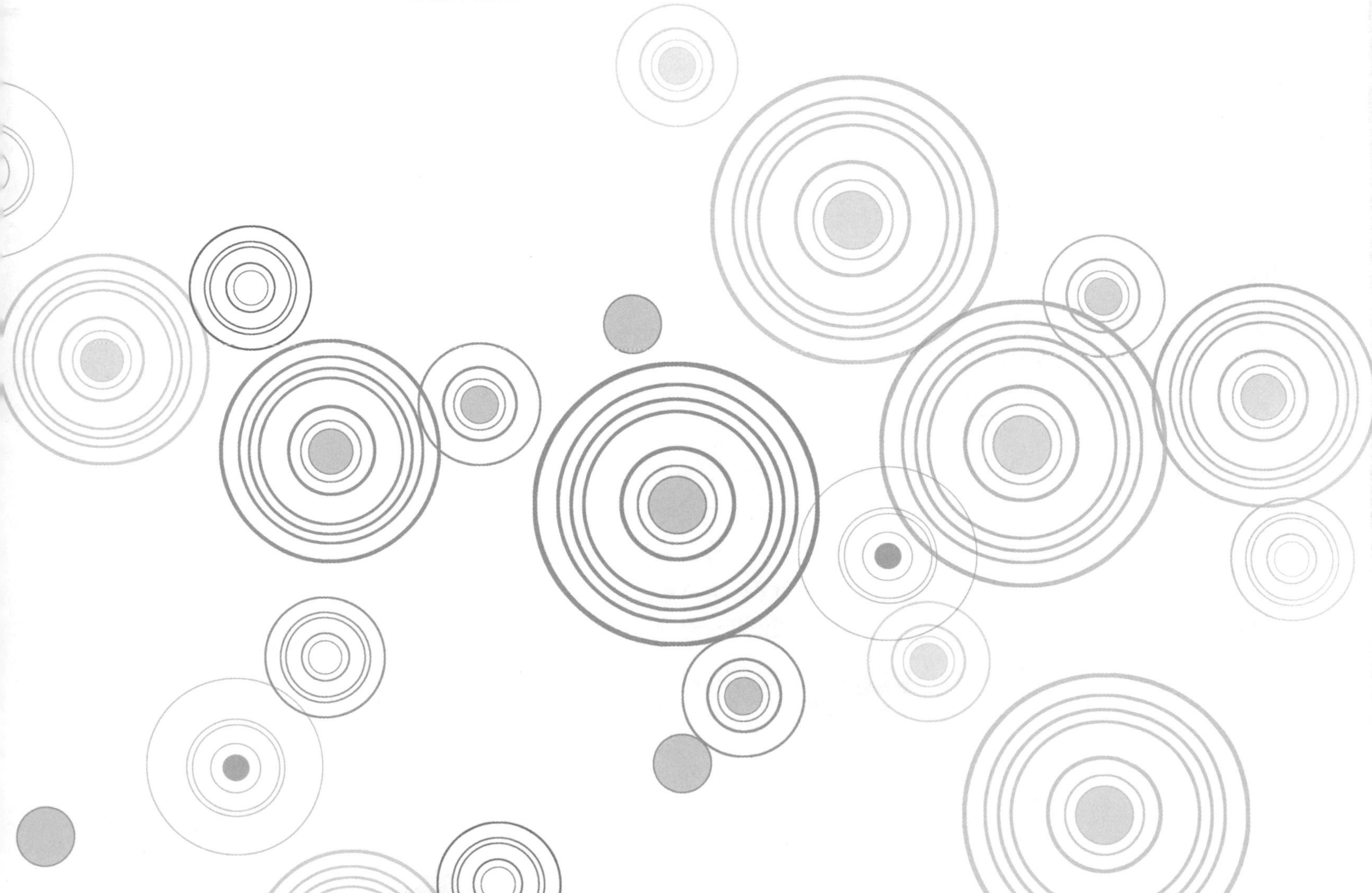

Meet Miley Cyrus

WE GOT THE PARTY

Words and Music by
KARA DioGUARDI

B♭
A♭/C
B♭/D
B♭
na do; it's all up to me and you.
Turn this

C
B♭
F
park in - to a club, the stars are lights and the moon is the vibe

B♭
F
C
B♭
from a - bove. This skate - board here's our ride, so pull on

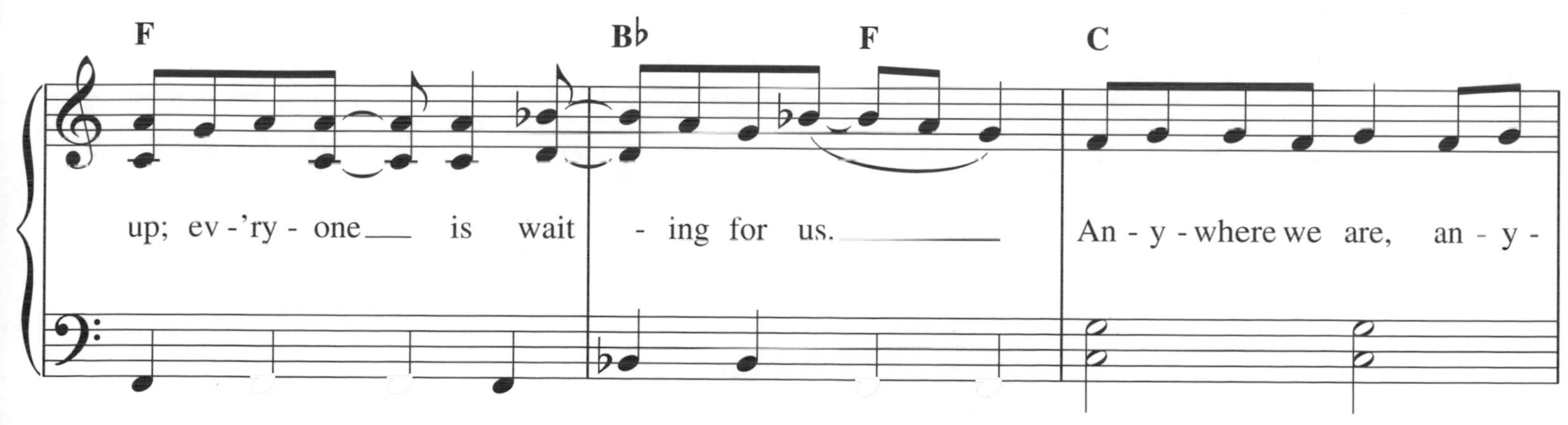
F
B♭
F
C
up; ev - 'ry - one is wait - ing for us. An - y - where we are, an - y -

B♭
F
B♭
F
where we go, ev - 'ry - bod - y
knows
we got the par - ty with us.

C
B♭
F
An - y - where we are, an - y -
where we go, ev - 'ry - bod - y
knows

To Coda
B♭
F
C
B♭
F
we got the par - ty with us.

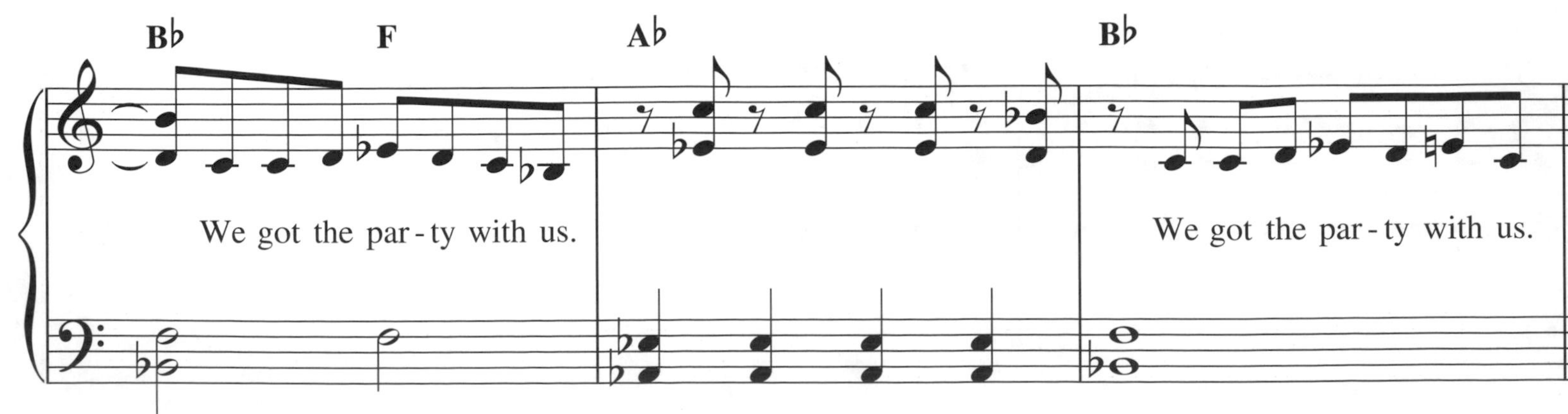
B♭
F
A♭
B♭
We got the par - ty with us.
We got the par - ty with us.

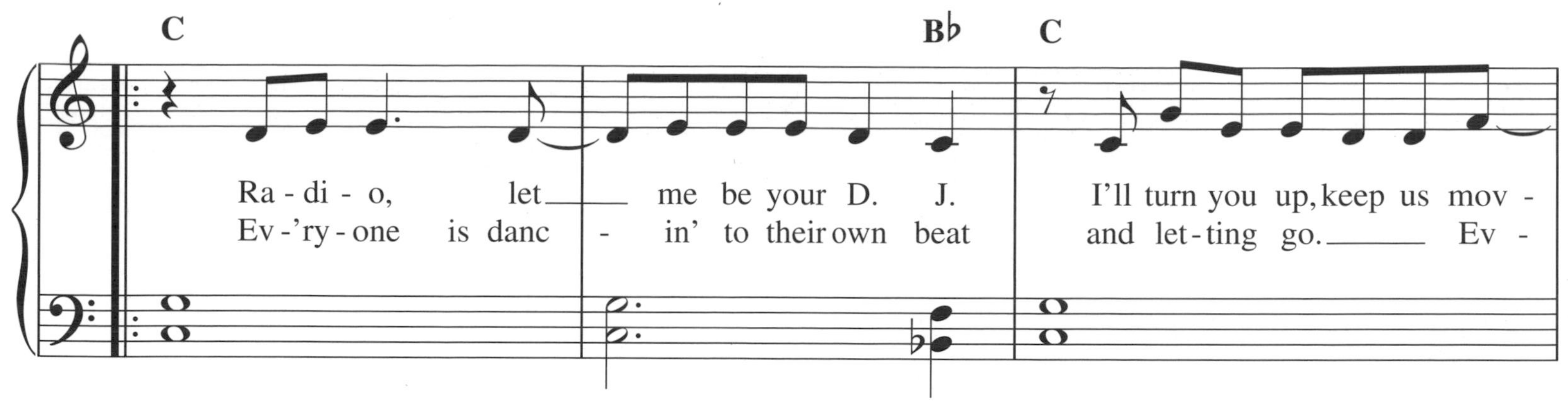
C
Bb
C
Ra - di - o, let me be your D. J. I'll turn you up, keep us mov -
Ev - 'ry - one is danc - in' to their own beat and let - ting go. Ev -

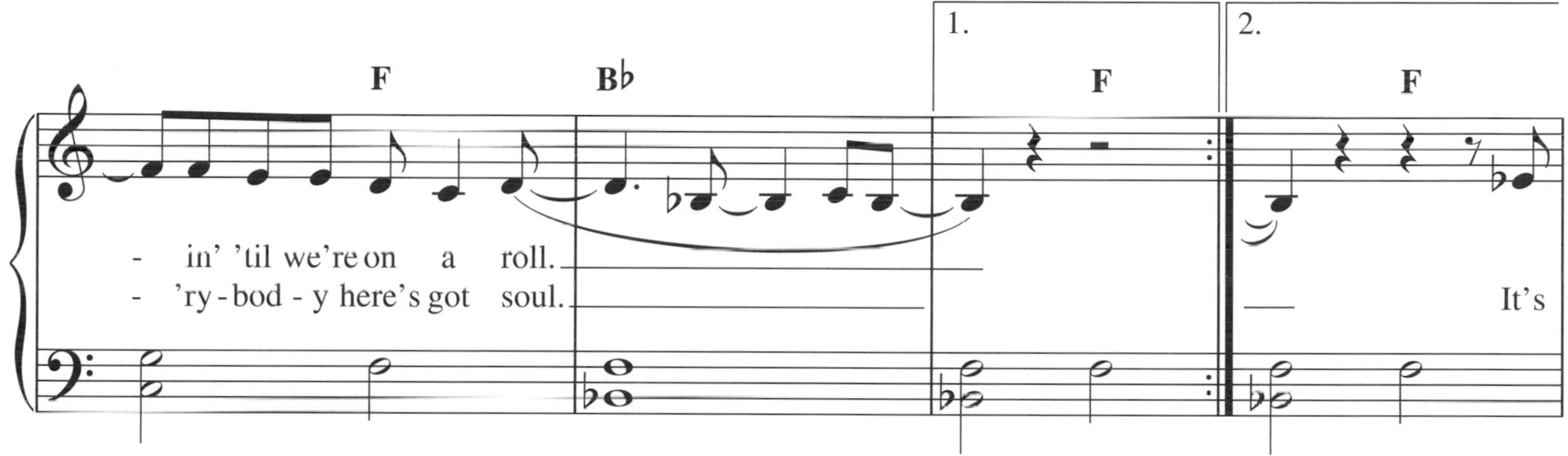
1.
2.
F
Bb
F
F
- in' 'til we're on a roll.
- 'ry - bod - y here's got soul.
It's

Ab
Bb
Ab
Fri - day and there's no - where to be. We're kick - in' it to - geth - er; it's so

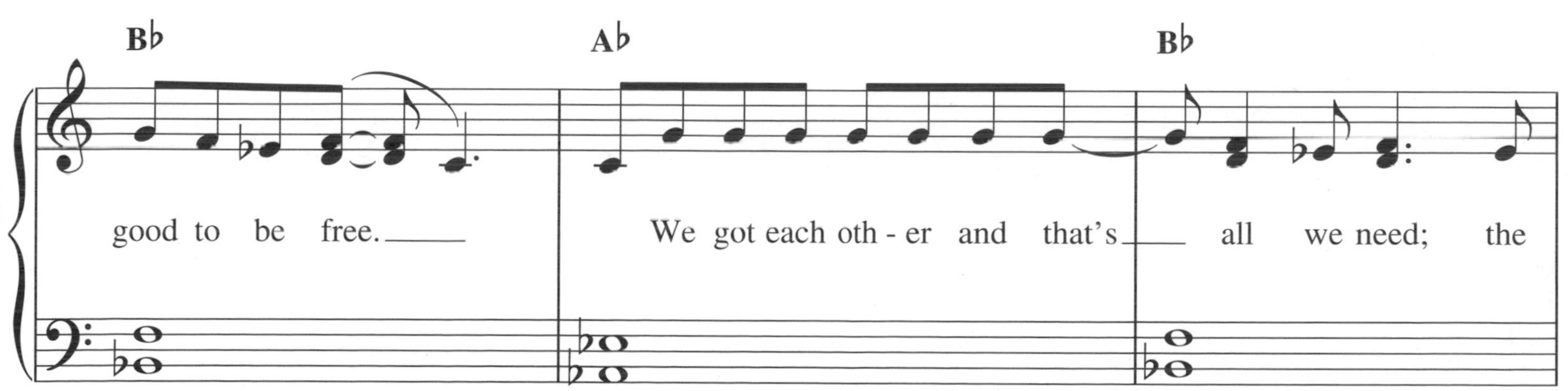
Bb
Ab
Bb
good to be free. We got each oth - er and that's all we need; the

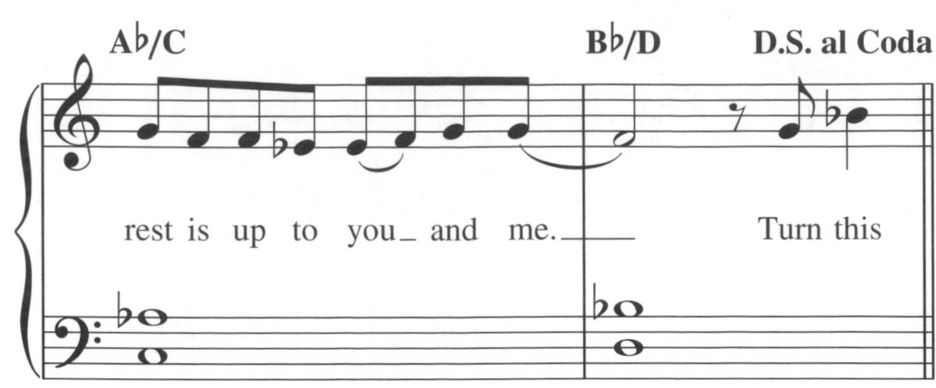

A♭/C
B♭/D
D.S. al Coda
rest is up to you and me.
Turn this

CODA
C

B♭
F
B♭
F
We got the par - ty with us.

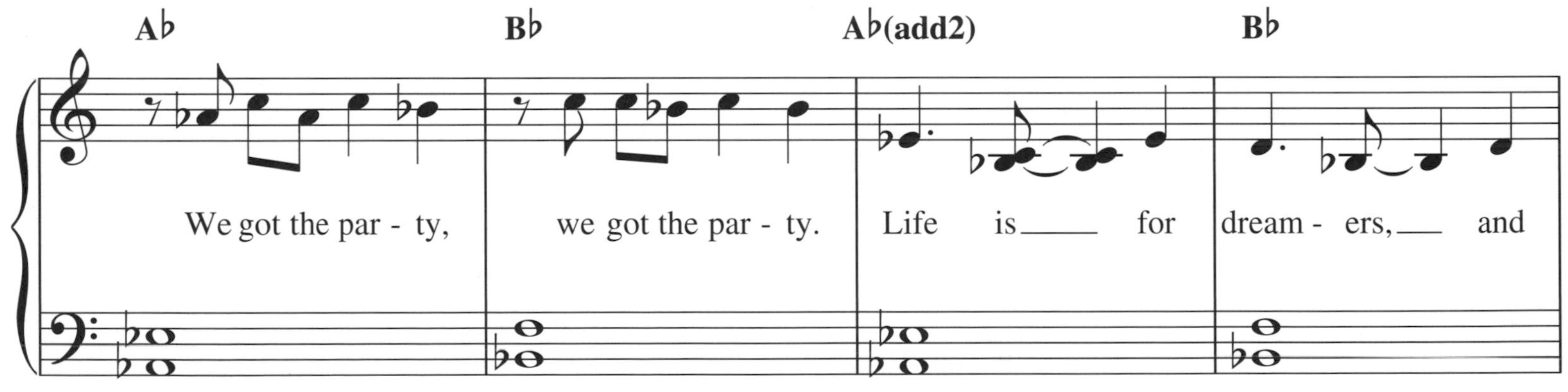

A♭
B♭
A♭(add2)
B♭
We got the par - ty,
we got the par - ty.
Life is for
dream - ers, and

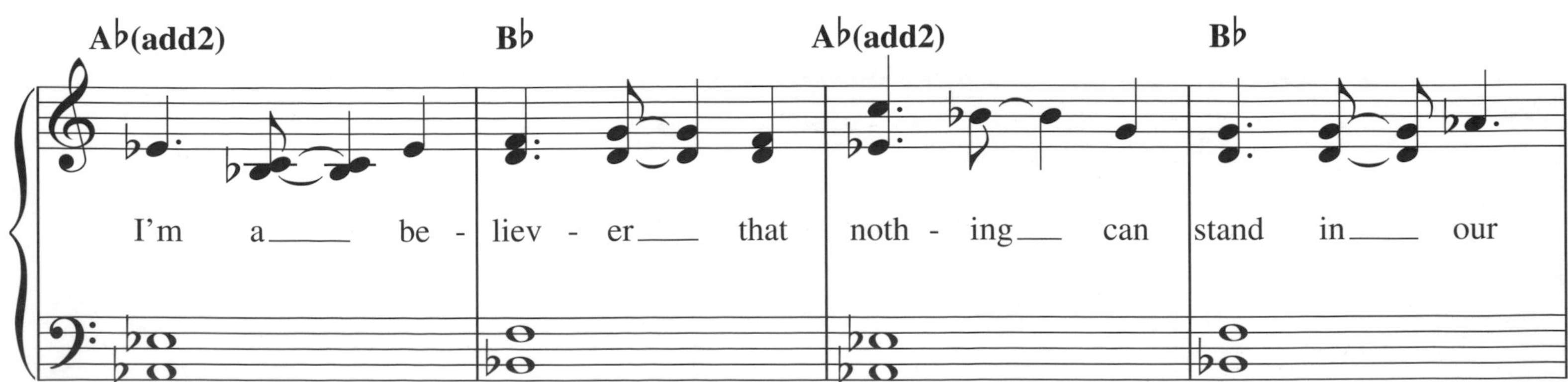

A♭(add2)
B♭
A♭(add2)
B♭
I'm a be -
liev - er that
noth - ing can
stand in our

A♭/C
B♭/D
B♭sus2
C
way to - day; let's find
a place to play.
Turn this
park in - to a

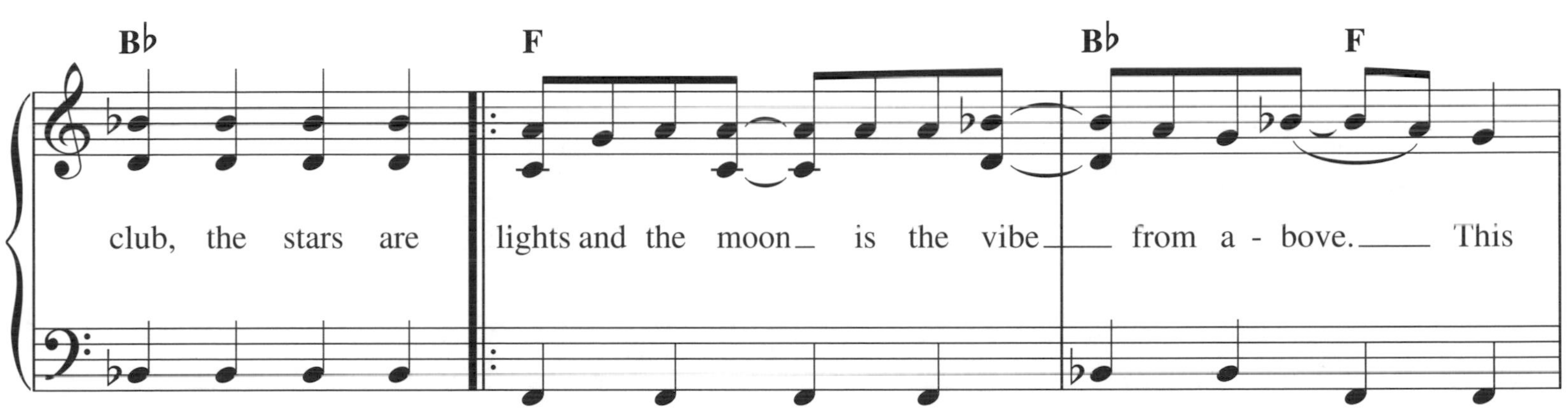
B♭
F
B♭
F
club, the stars are
lights and the moon is the vibe
from a - bove. This

C
B♭
F
skate - board here's our
ride, so pull on
up; ev - 'ry - one is wait -

B♭
F
C
B♭
F
- ing for us.
An-y-where we are, an-y-
where we go, ev-'ry-bod - y
knows

B♭
F
C
B♭
we got the par - ty with us.
An - y - where we are, an - y -
where we go, ev - 'ry - bod - y

1.
F
B♭
C
B♭
knows.
Turn this
park in - to a
club, the stars are

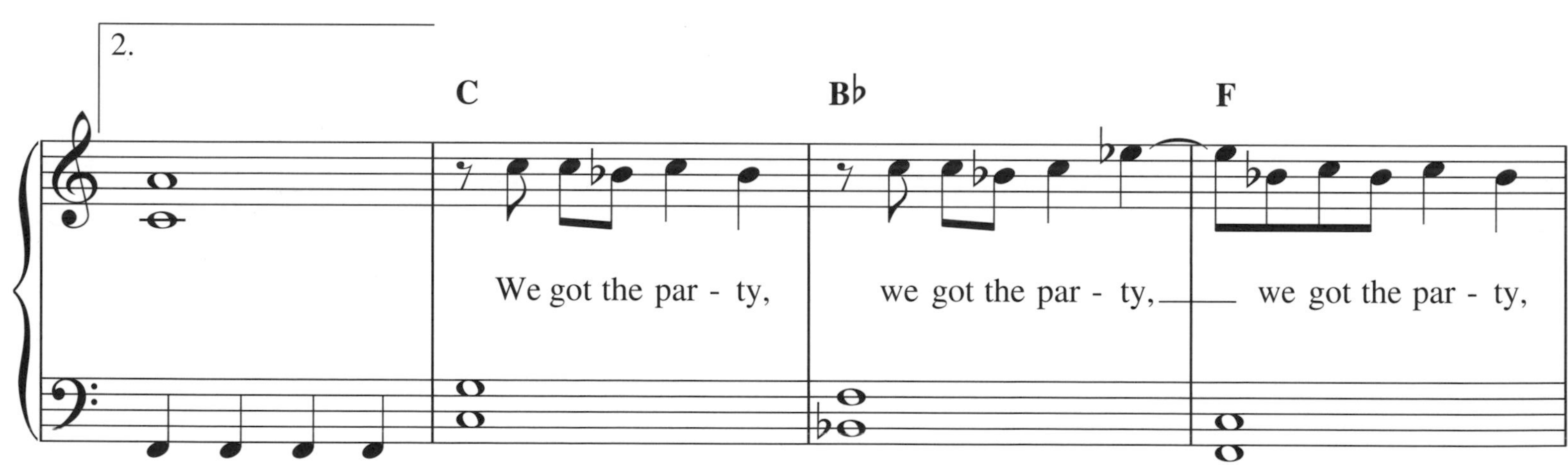

2.
C
B♭
F
We got the par - ty,
we got the par - ty,
we got the par - ty,

B♭
F
A♭
B♭
C
we got the par - ty with us.
We got the par - ty with us.

NOBODY'S PERFECT

Words and Music by MATTHEW GERRARD
and ROBBIE NEVIL

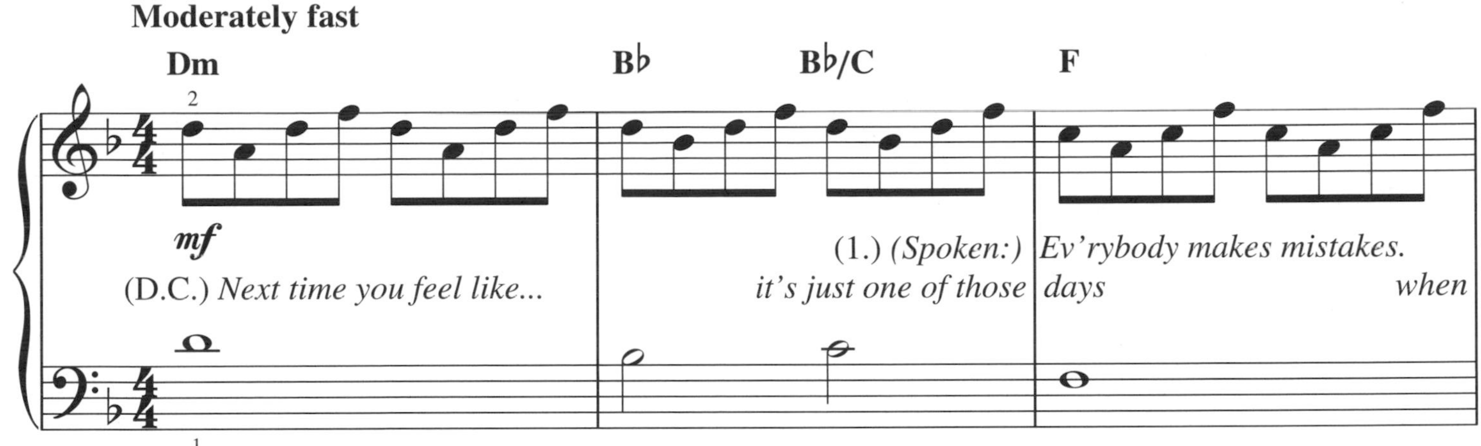

2.
C
Cm
E♭
Ev'rybody gets that way.
Some - times I'm in a jam;
Some - times I work a scheme,
I've got - ta make a plan.
but then it flips on me;

A♭
B♭
It might be cra - zy;
does - n't turn out how I planned,
I do it an - y - way.
gets stuck in quick - sand.

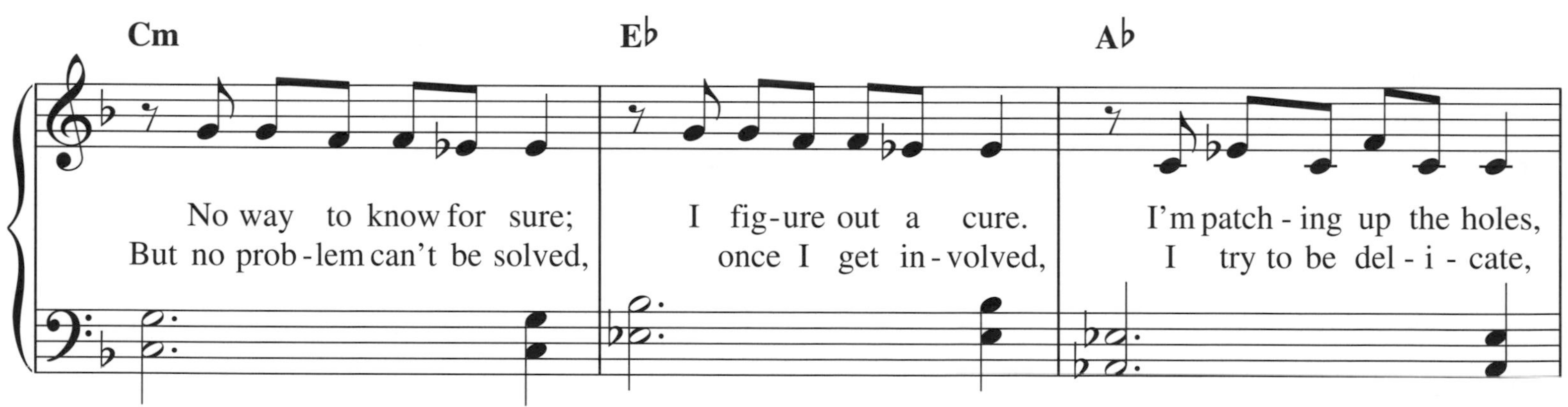
Cm
E♭
A♭
No way to know for sure;
But no prob - lem can't be solved,
I fig - ure out a cure.
once I get in - volved,
I'm patch - ing up the holes,
I try to be del - i - cate,

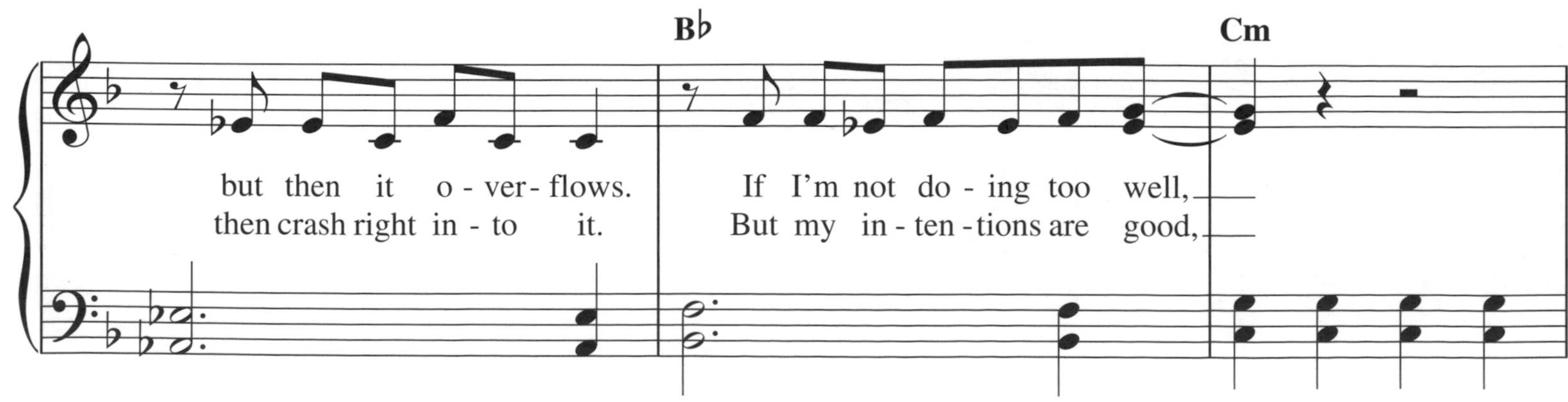
B♭
Cm
but then it o - ver - flows.
then crash right in - to it.
If I'm not do - ing too well,
But my in - ten - tions are good,

B♭
C
Dm
why be so hard on my - self?
some - times just mis - un - der - stood.
No - bod - y's per - fect. I got - ta work

B♭
F
C
it a - gain and a - gain, 'til I get it right.
No - bod - y's per -

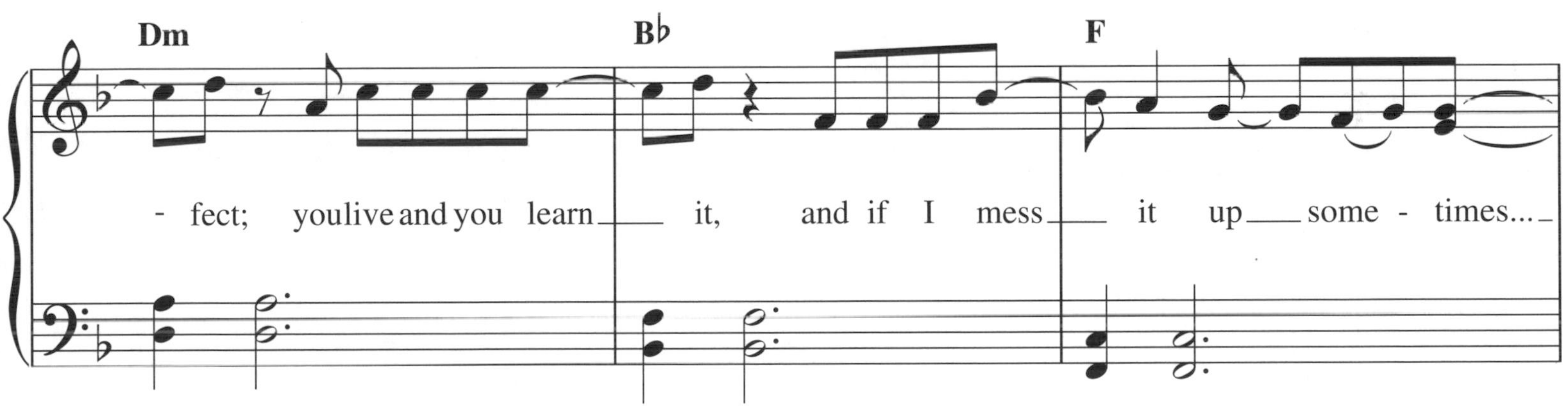
Dm
B♭
F
- fect; you live and you learn it, and if I mess it up some - times...

1.
C
B♭
No - bod - y's per - fect.

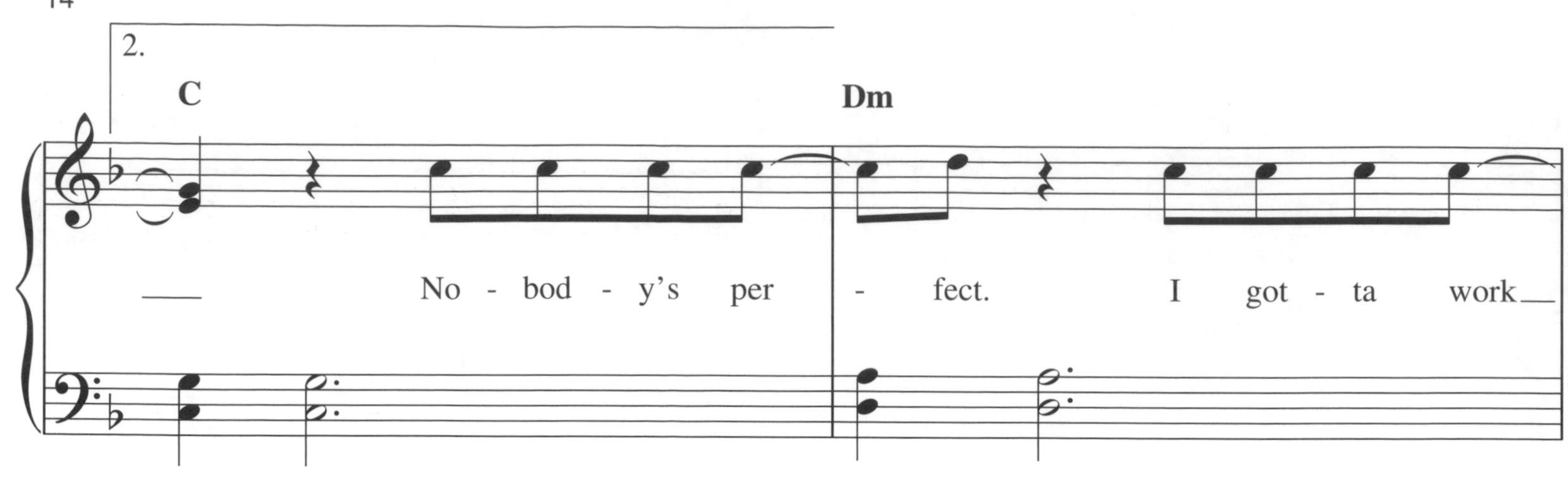
2.
C
Dm
No - bod - y's per - fect. I got - ta work

B♭
F
C
it; I know in time I'll find a way. No-bod-y's per -

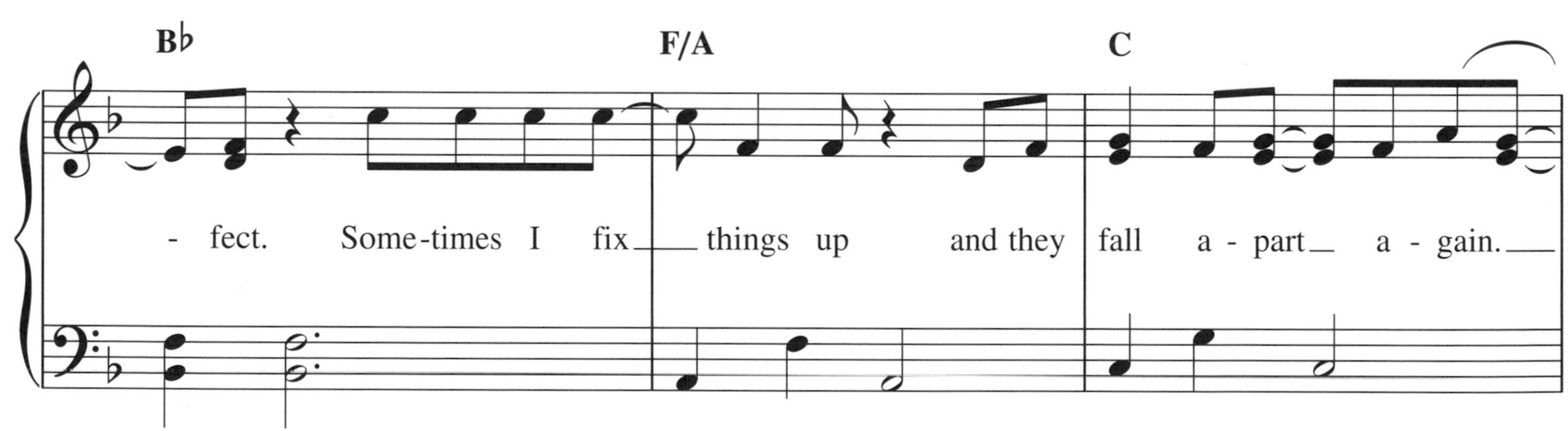
B♭
F/A
C
- fect. Some-times I fix things up and they fall a - part a - gain.

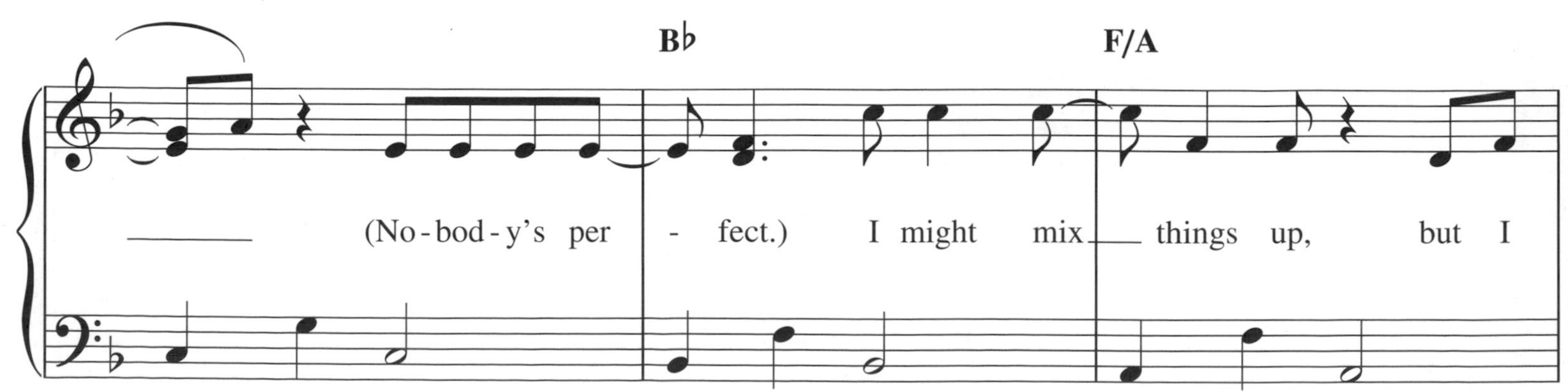
B♭
F/A
(No-bod-y's per - fect.) I might mix things up, but I

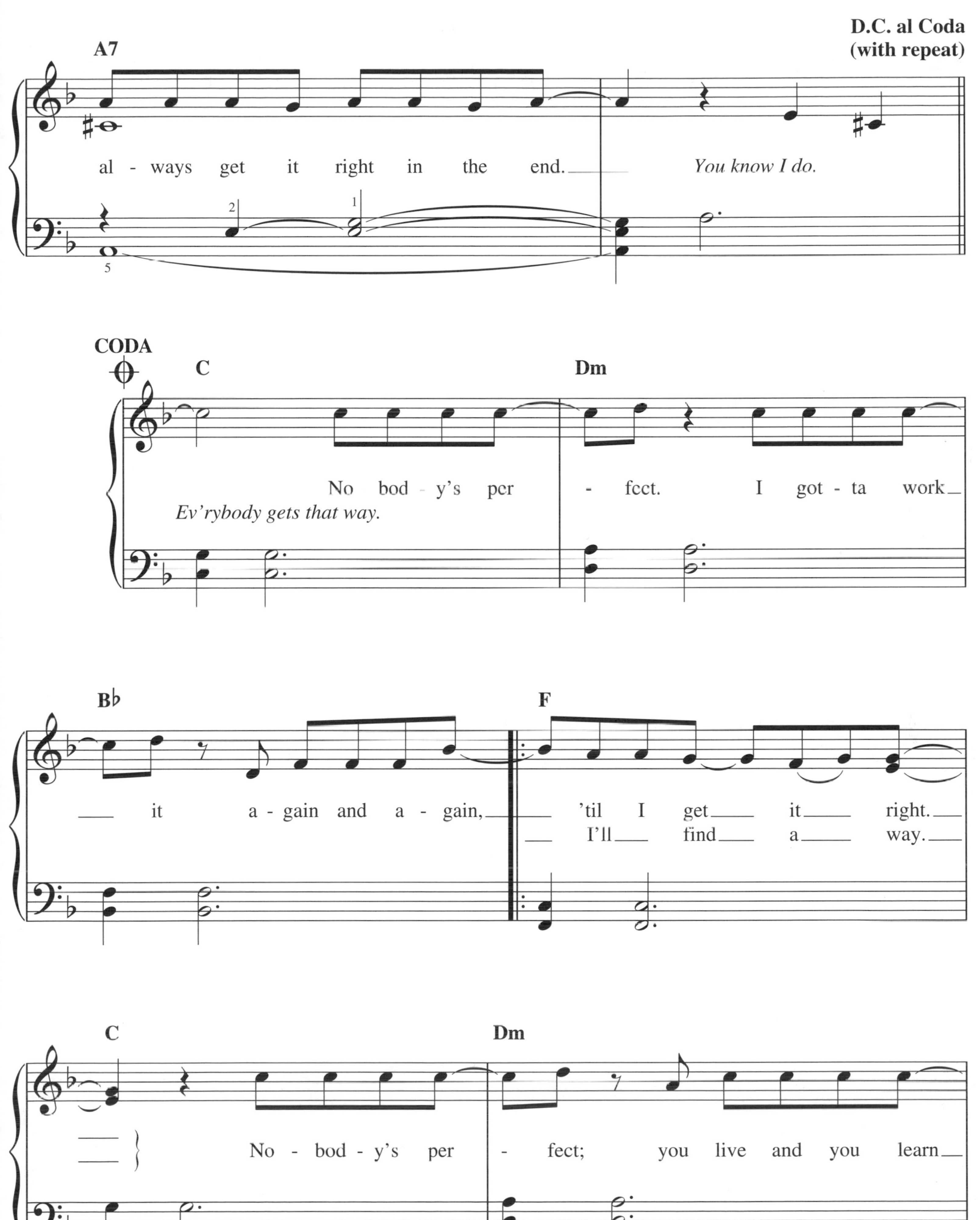
D.C. al Coda
(with repeat)
A7
al - ways get it right in the end.
You know I do.
CODA
C
Dm
No bod - y's per - fect. I got - ta work
Ev'rybody gets that way.
B♭
F
it a - gain and a - gain, 'til I get it right.
I'll find a way.
C
Dm
No - bod - y's per - fect; you live and you learn

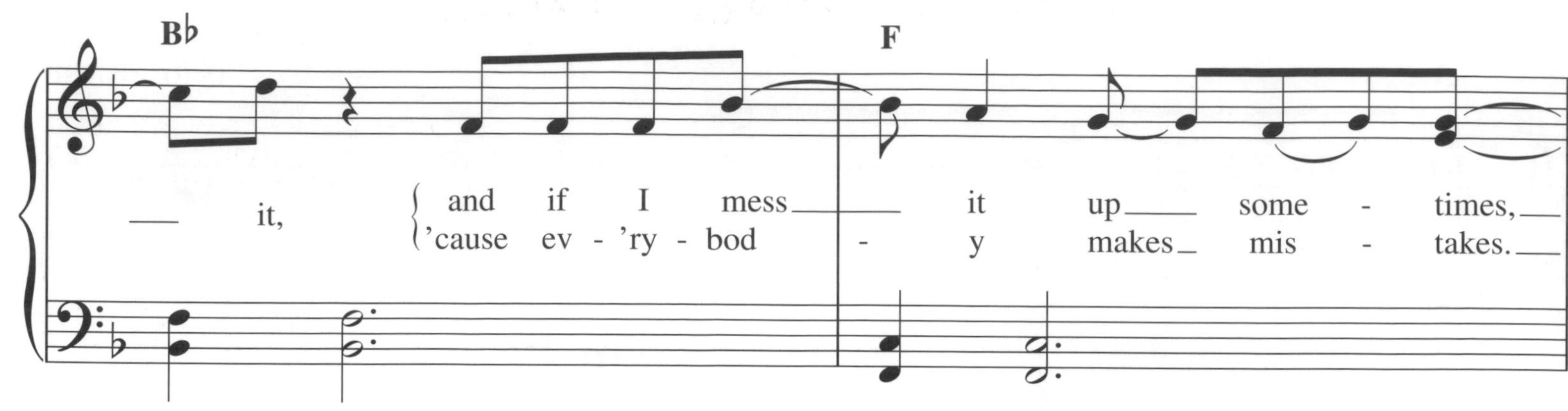
B♭
F
it,
and if I mess
'cause ev - 'ry - bod
- y
it up
makes
some - times,
mis - takes.

1.
C
Dm
B♭
no-bod-y's per - fect. I got-ta work it. I know in time

2.
C
B♭
F/A
No-bod-y's per - fect. No - bod-y's per - fect.

Gm
C
Dm
No - bod - y's per - fect.

MAKE SOME NOISE

Words and Music by ANDY DODD
and ADAM WATTS

Em
D(add4)
C
G
Em
D(add4)
May - be it's your time to lift off and fly; you won't know if you nev - er
You have a dia-mond in - side of your heart, a light that shines bright as the

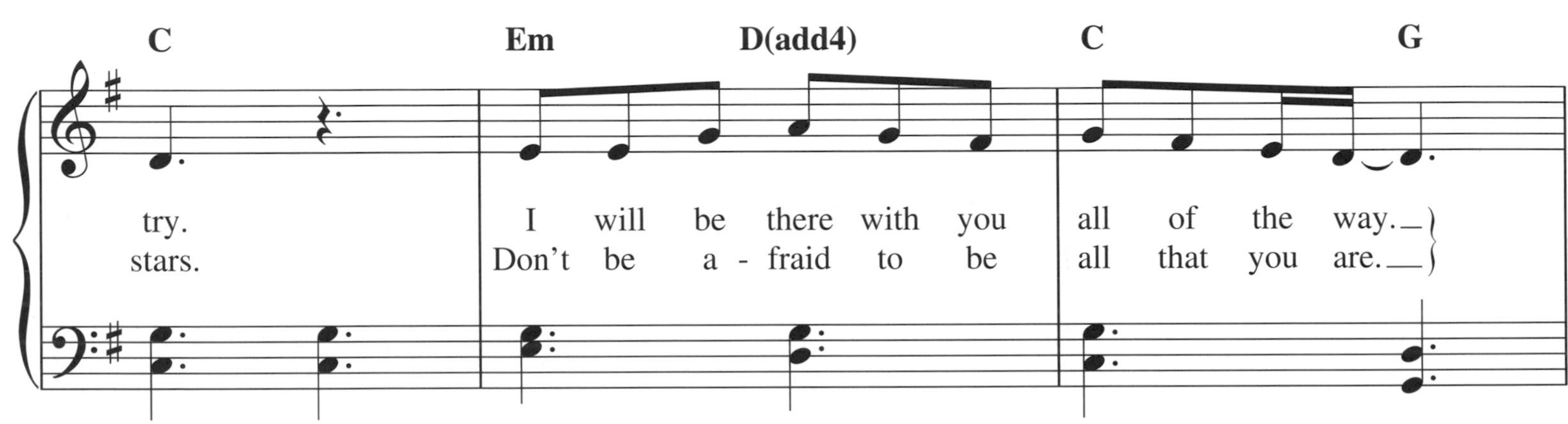
C
Em
D(add4)
C
G
try. I will be there with you all of the way.
stars. Don't be a - fraid to be all that you are.

A7
Csus2
G
Csus2
You'll be fine. Don't let an - y - one tell you that

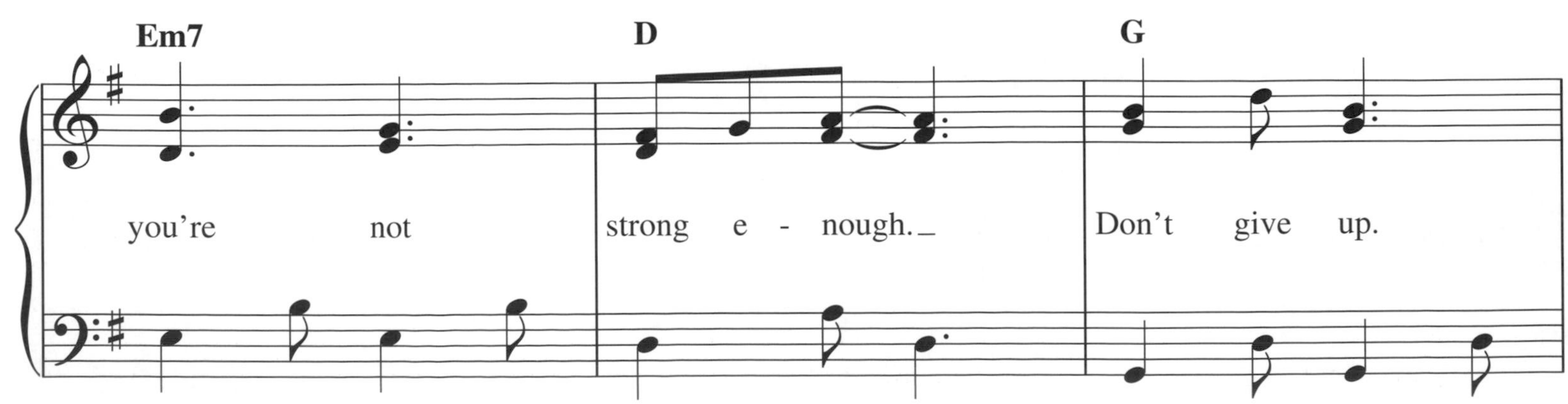
Em7
D
G
you're not strong e - nough. Don't give up.

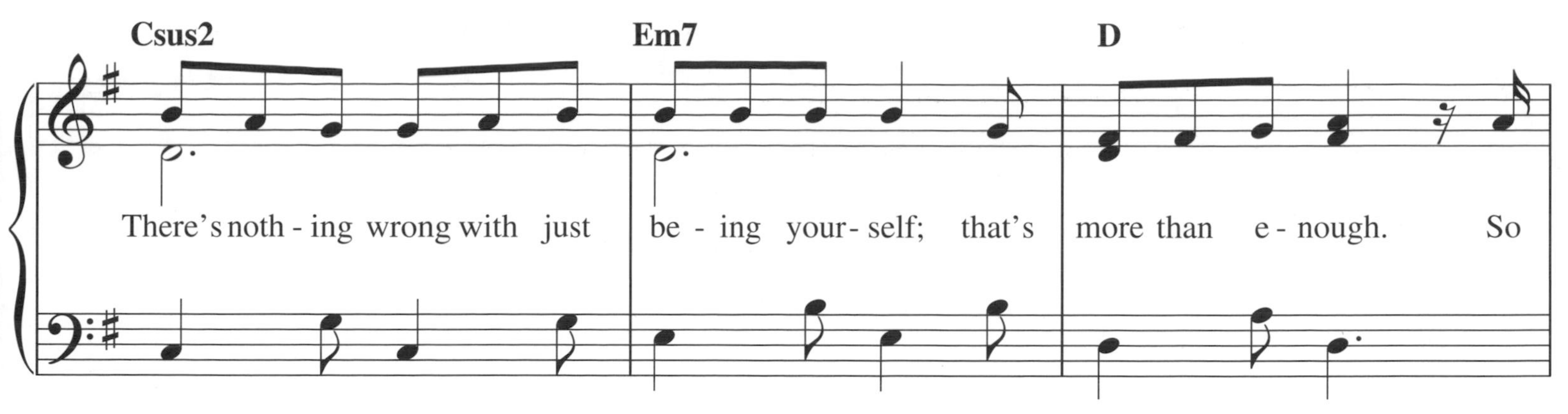
Csus2
Em7
D
There's noth - ing wrong with just
be - ing your - self; that's
more than e - nough. So

C
D
Em7
Csus2
G
come on and raise your voice,
speak your mind and make some noise,

To Coda
A7
G
Csus2
and sing...
Hey, hey,
make some noise.
Hey, hey,

1.
2.
Em7
D
Em7
D
C
G
yeah. You
yeah.
You can't just sit back and

D Em7 C G D
watch the world change; it mat - ters what you've got to say.

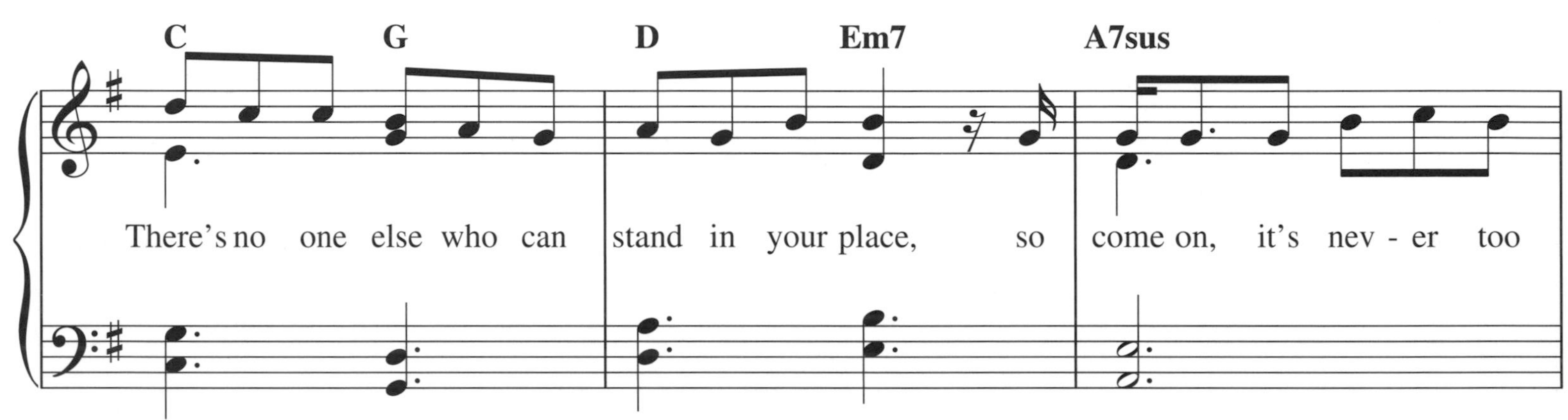
C G D Em7 A7sus
There's no one else who can stand in your place, so come on, it's nev - er too

Csus2 Em D(add4) C G
late. May - be it's your time to lift off and fly. You

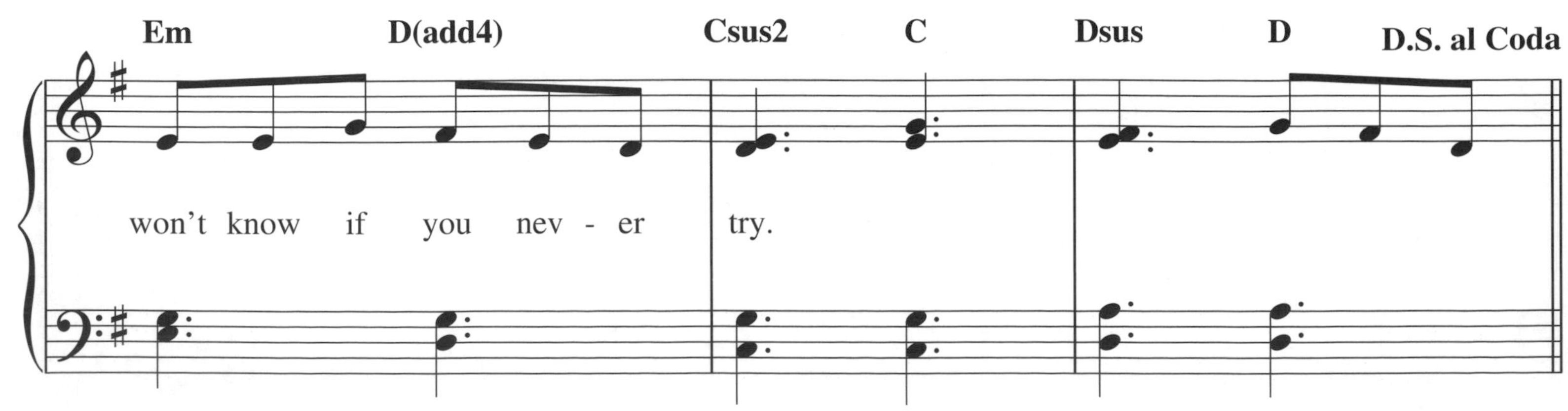
Em D(add4) Csus2 C Dsus D
D.S. al Coda
won't know if you nev - er try.

CODA
G
1.
C
Em7
D
Hey, hey, make some noise. Hey, hey, yeah.
2.
Csus2
Em7
D
G/B
Speak your mind and make some noise, and sing... Hey, yeah,
Csus2
G/B
1.
D
2.
D
hey, yeah, hey, yeah, make some noise. make some noise.
G/B
Csus2
G
D
G5
rit.

ROCK STAR

Words and Music by JEANNIE LURIE,
ARIS ARCHONTIS and CHEN NEEMAN

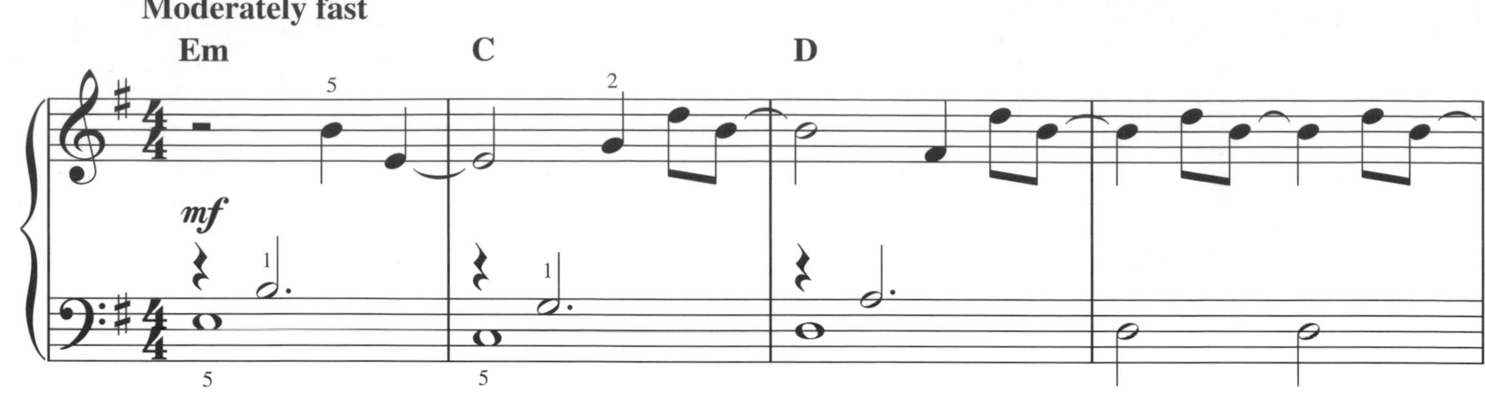

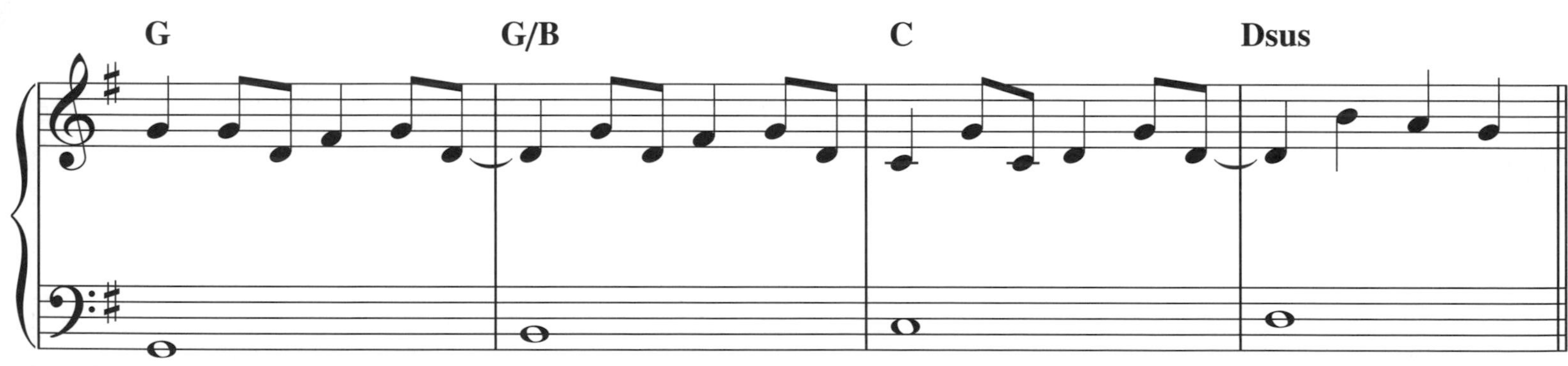

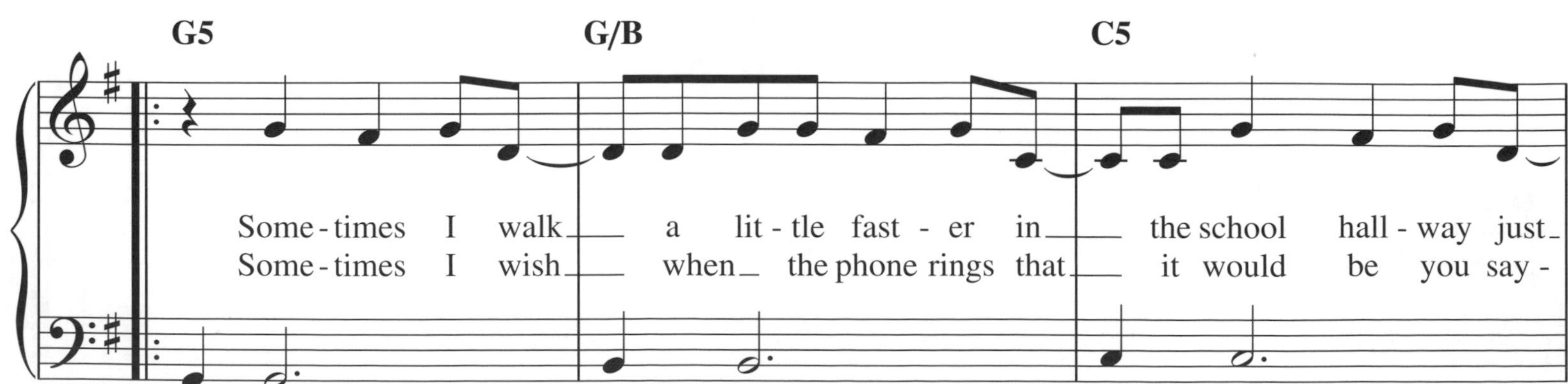

D5
G5
G/B
to get next to you. Some days I spend a lit - tle ex - tra time
- in', "Let's hang out," then you con - fess that there's some-thing spe -

C5
D5
Em
in the morn - ing, dress to im - press you. Guess you don't no - tice, guess
- cial be - tween us. Why don't we find out? You don't e - ven know me. Guess

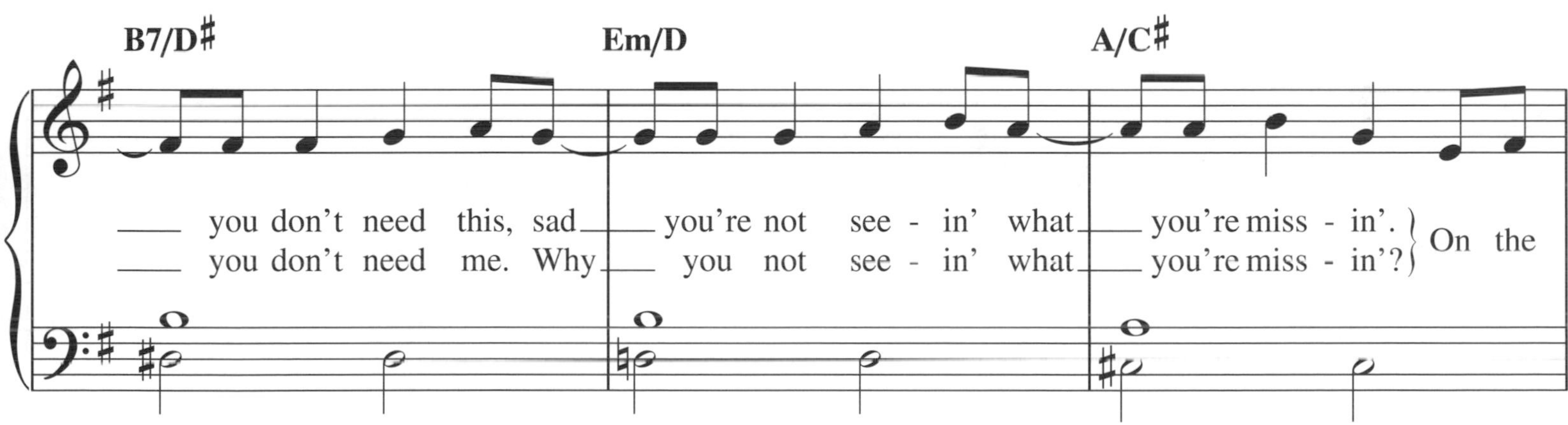
B7/D♯
Em/D
A/C♯
you don't need this, sad you're not see - in' what you're miss - in'.
you don't need me. Why you not see - in' what you're miss - in'?
On the

G/C
D5
out - side, shy - in' a - way; on the in - side, dy - in' to say

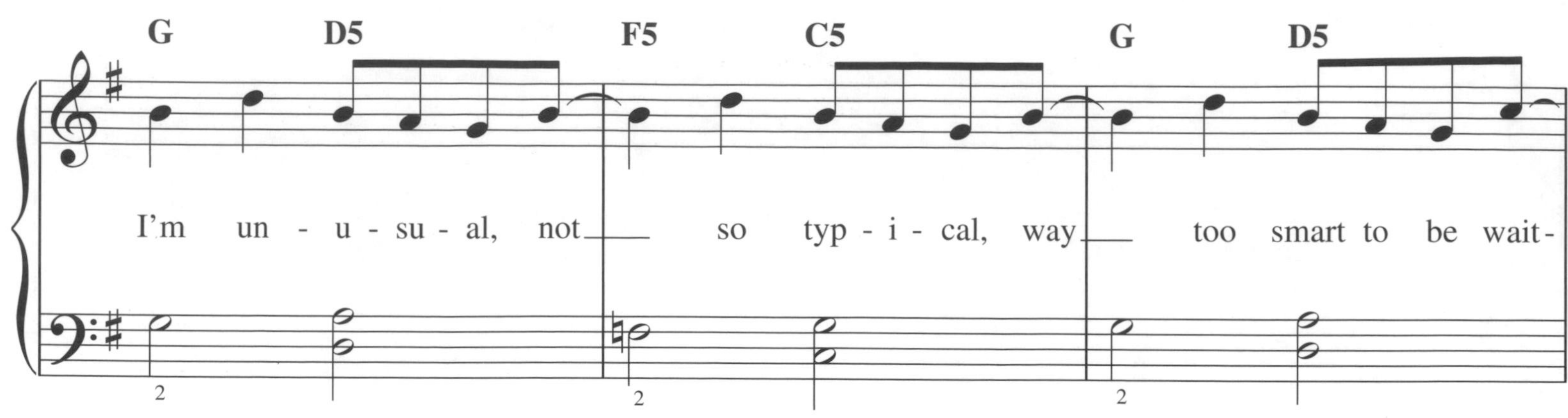
G
D5
F5
C5
G
D5
I'm un - u - su - al, not so typ - i - cal, way too smart to be wait-

F5
C5
G
D5
F5
C5
- ing a - round. Tai Chi prac - tic - in', snow - board cham - pi - on,

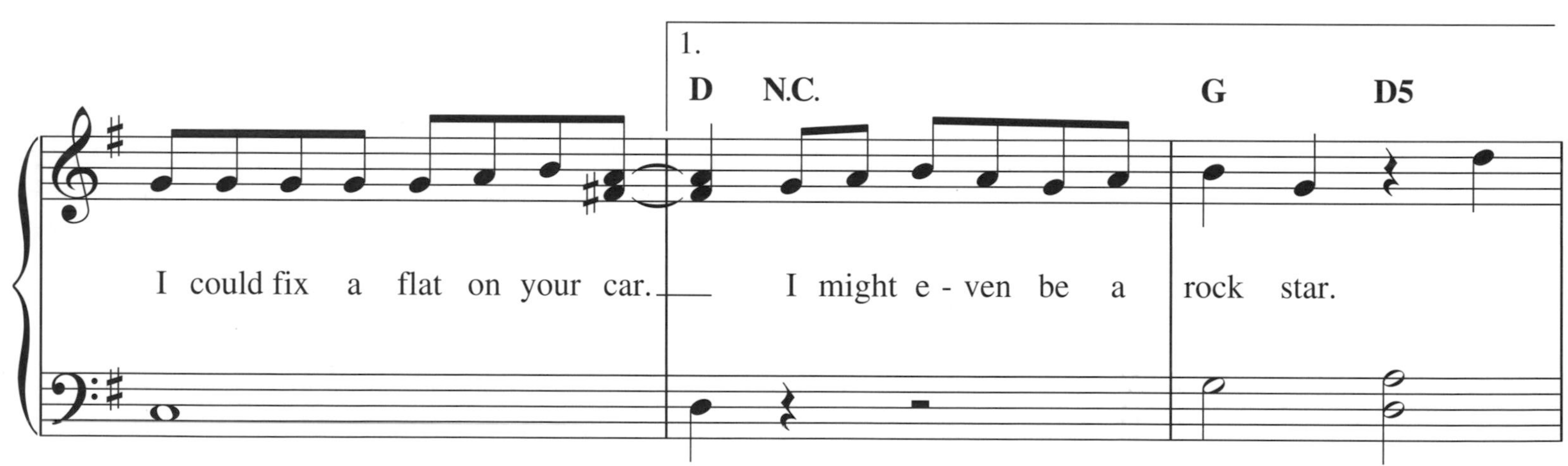
1.
D
N.C.
G
D5
I could fix a flat on your car. I might e - ven be a rock star.

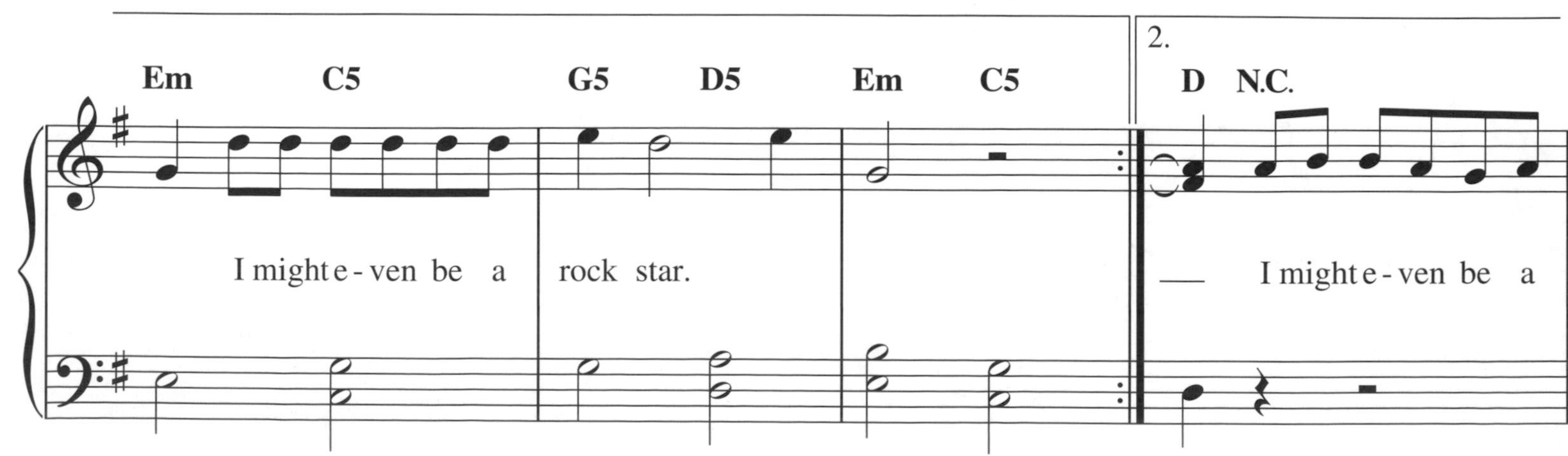
Em
C5
G5
D5
Em
C5
2.
D
N.C.
I might e - ven be a rock star. I might e - ven be a

Em
C
D
rock star.
If you on - ly
knew the real me,

Em
C
I might e - ven be a
rock star.
I'm tell - ing you that

A
C
we are meant to be,
that would - n't it be
nice if you could see

D
G
G/B
C5
that I real - ly am a
rock star,
yeah, yeah?

Dsus
G
E♭
Yeah, I real-ly am a rock star.

Dsus
G5
D5
Em
C5
E♭5

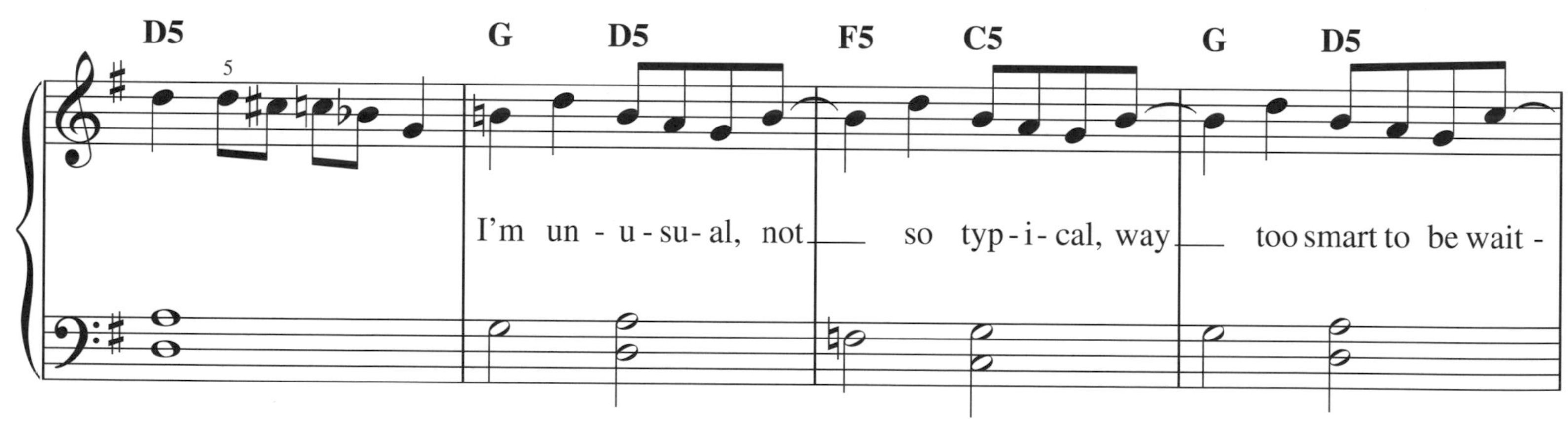
D5
G
D5
F5
C5
G
D5
I'm un - u - su - al, not so typ - i - cal, way too smart to be wait -

F5
C5
G
D5
F5
C5
- ing a - round. Tai Chi prac - tic - in', snow - board cham - pi - on,

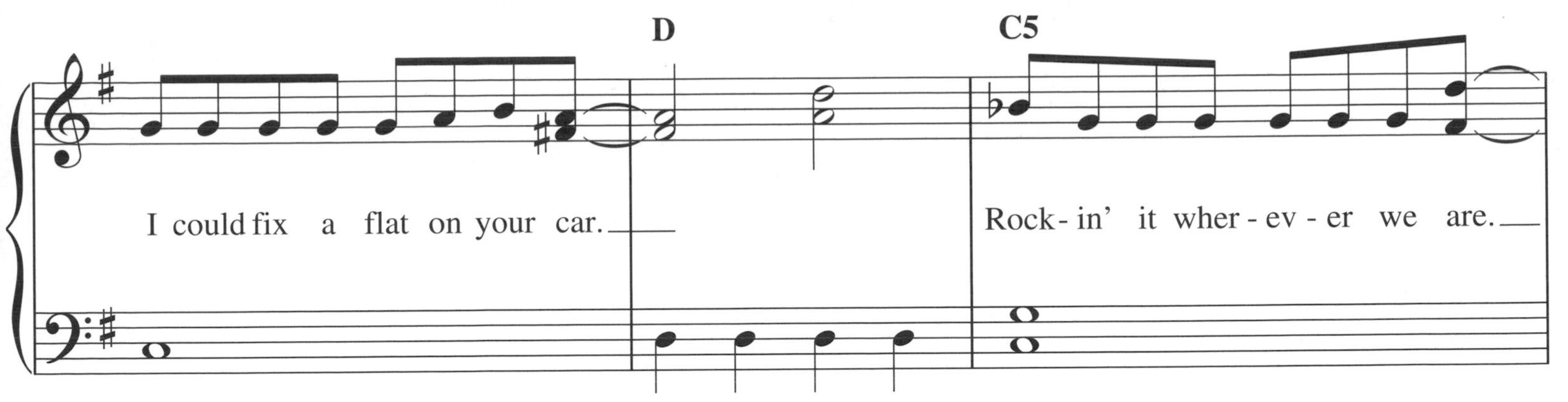
D
C5
I could fix a flat on your car.
Rock-in' it wher-ev-er we are.

D
D5
G
D5
Yeah, yeah, that I real-ly am a rock star,

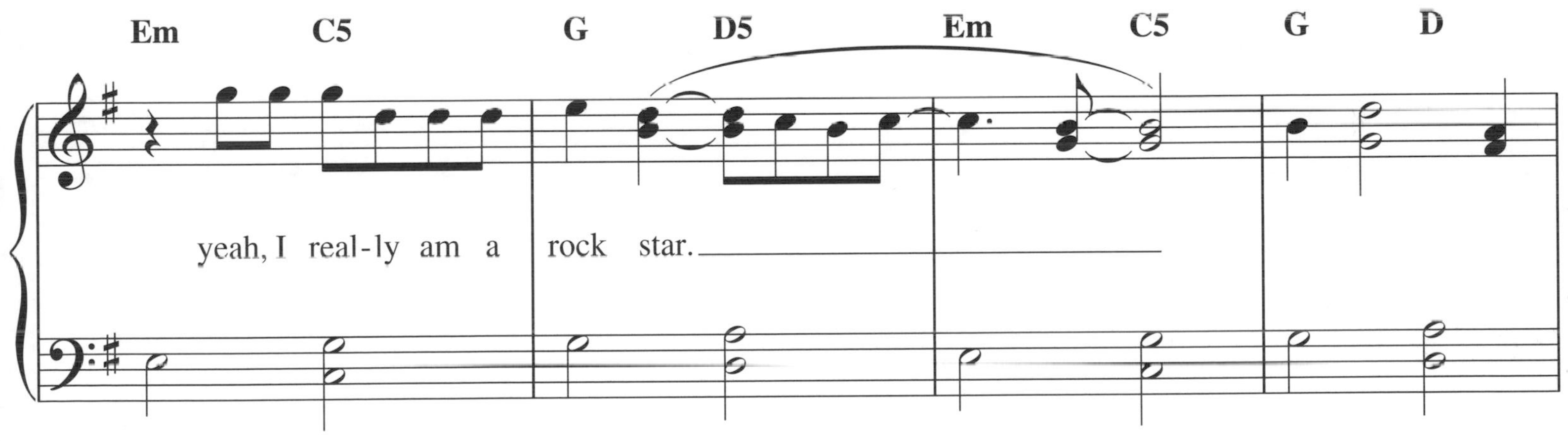
Em
C5
G
D5
Em
C5
G
D
yeah, I real-ly am a rock star.

Em
C
G
D
Em
C5
G
I am a rock star. Whoa-oh - oh - oh.

OLD BLUE JEANS

Words and Music by MICHAEL BRADFORD
and PAM SHEYNE

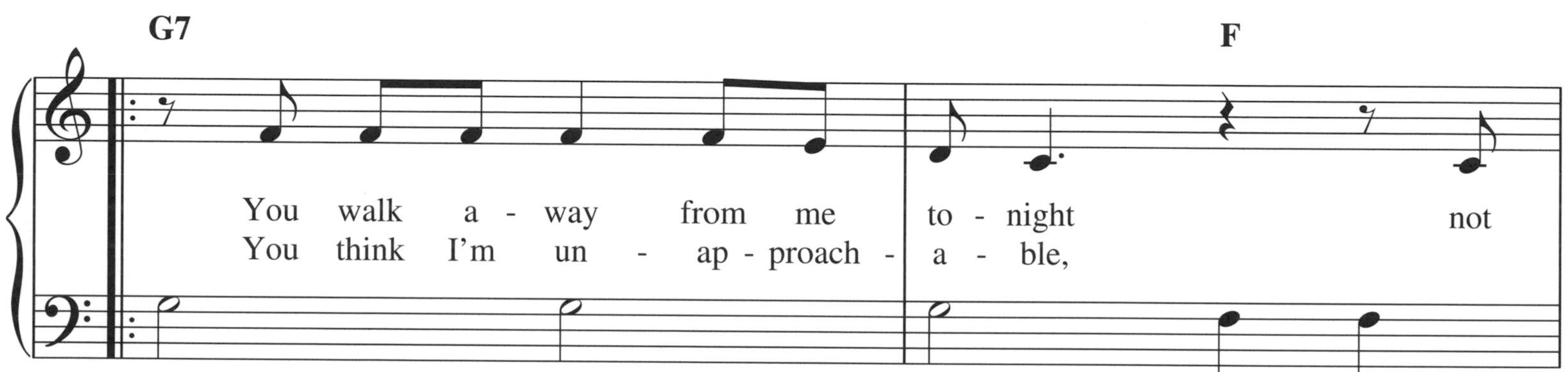

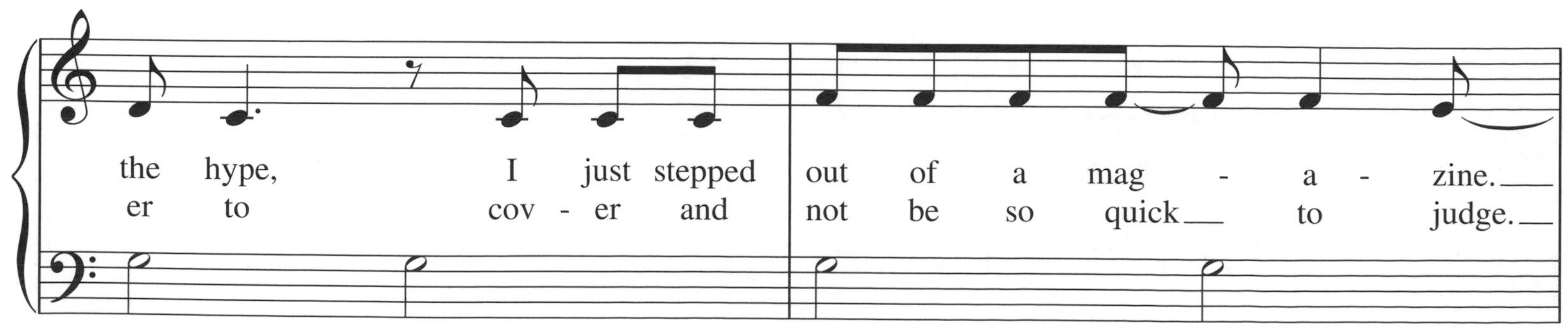

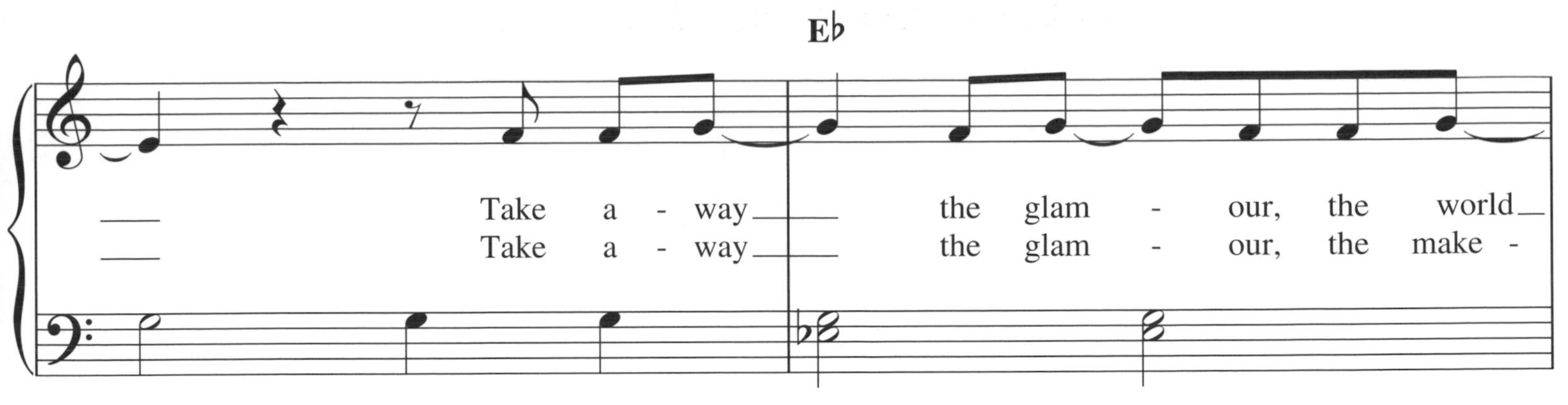
E♭
Take a - way the glam - our, the world
Take a - way the glam - our, the make -

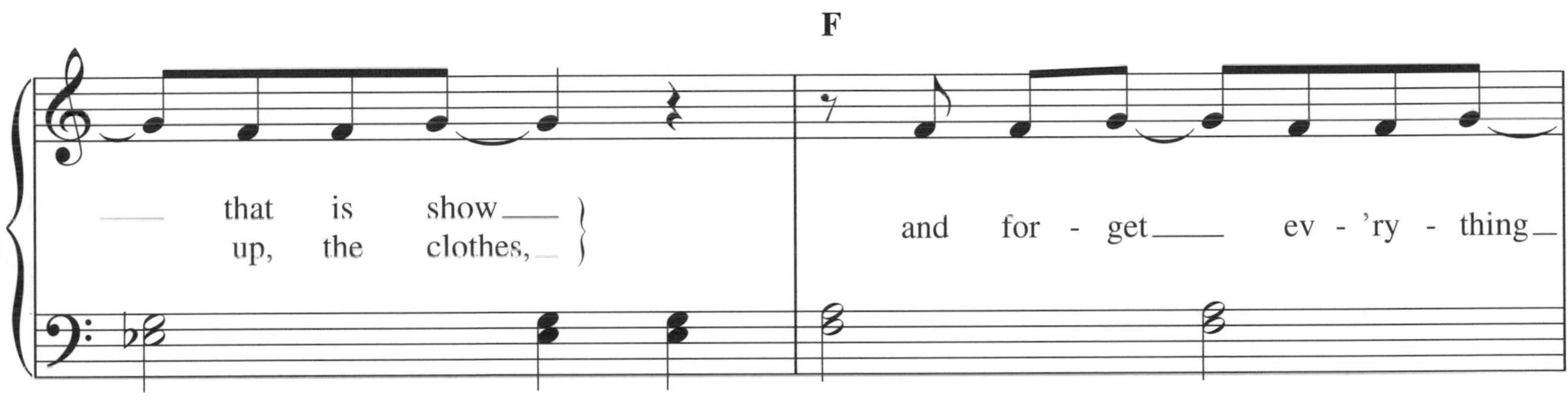
F
that is show
up, the clothes,
and for - get ev - 'ry - thing

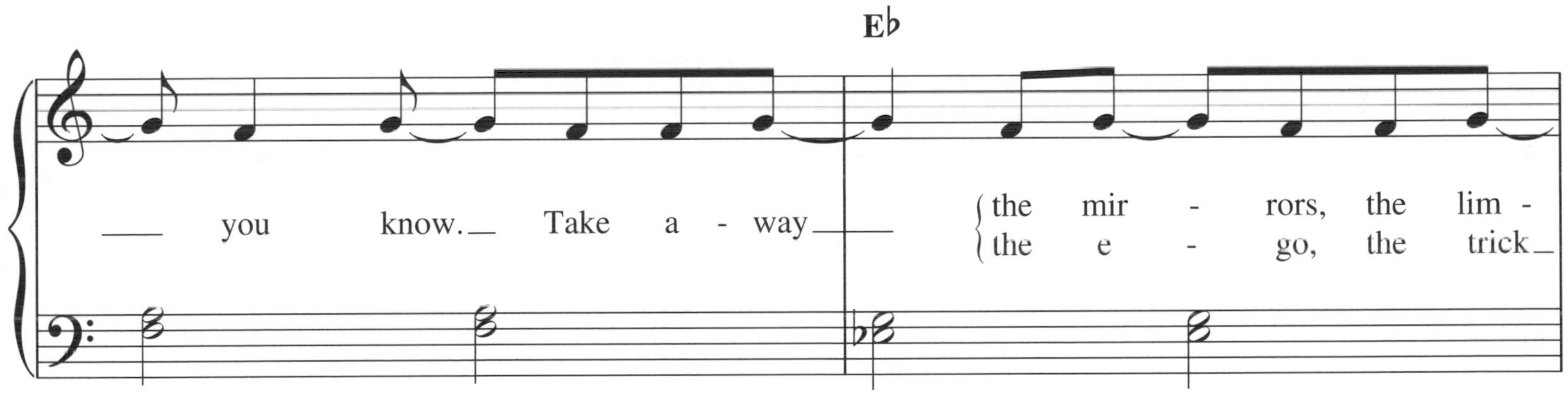
E♭
you know. Take a - way
the mir - rors, the lim -
the e - go, the trick

D
- o, the lights,
of the light,
'cause I don't wan - na dress up

G
F
to - night. I'm gon - na
put on my old blue jeans,

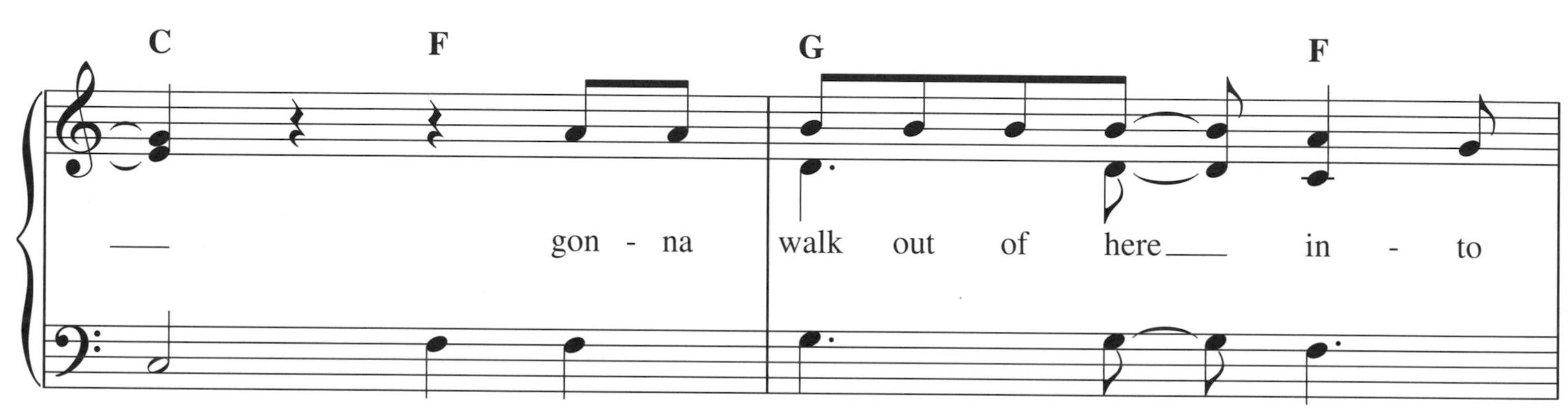
C
F
G
F
gon - na
walk out of here in - to

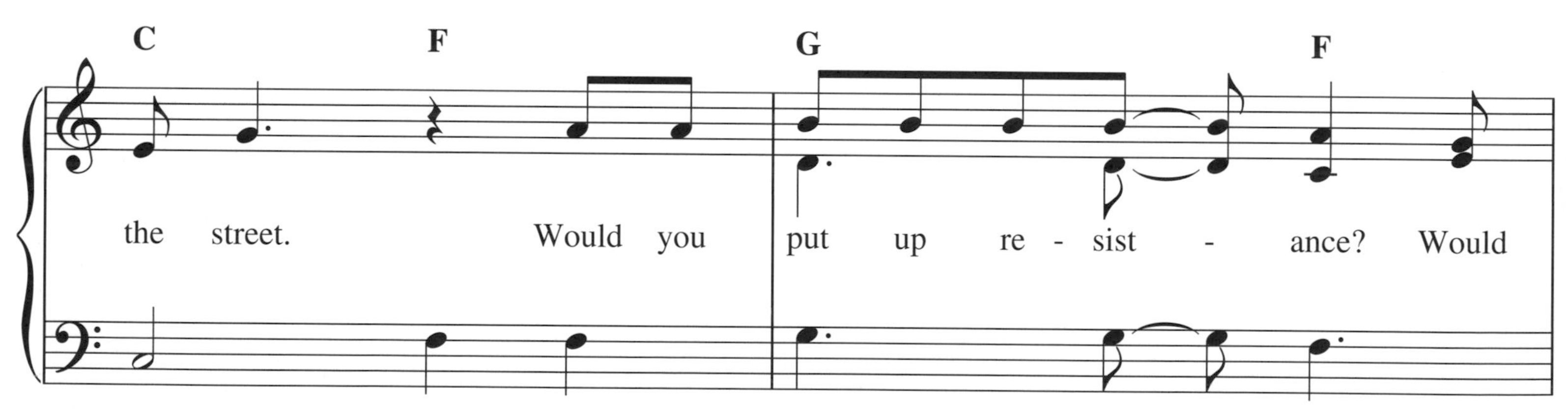
C
F
G
F
the street. Would you
put up re - sist - ance? Would

C
F
G
F
it make a dif - f'rence? Would
you know the real me,

1.
C
F
G
F
G
me in my old__ blue jeans?___

F
2.
C
F
G
F
me in my old?.... I'm gon - na
put on my old__ blue jeans,_

C
F
G
F
C
F
___ gon - na
walk out of here__ in - to
the street. Would you

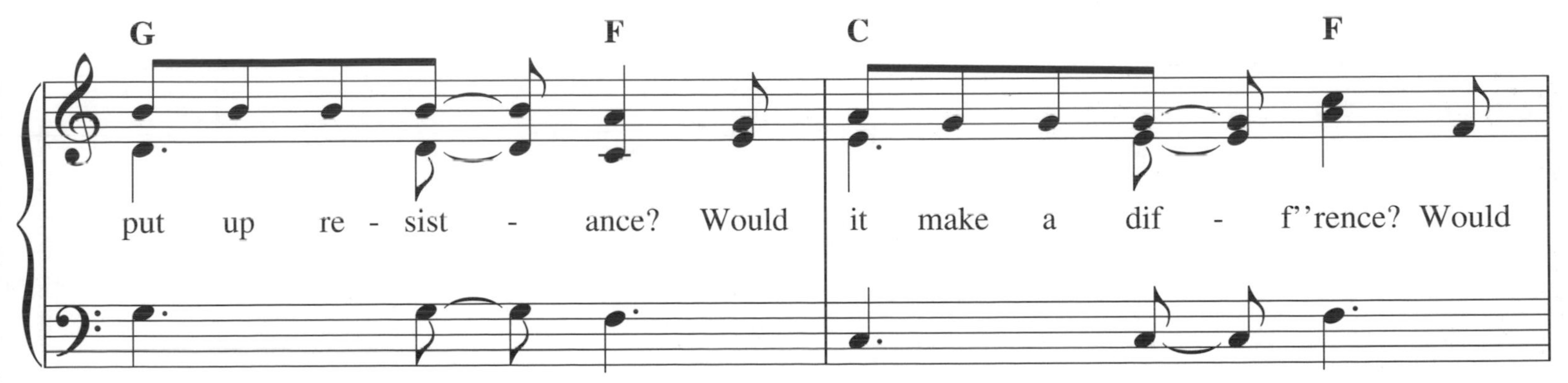
G
F
C
F
put up re - sist - ance? Would
it make a dif - f''rence? Would

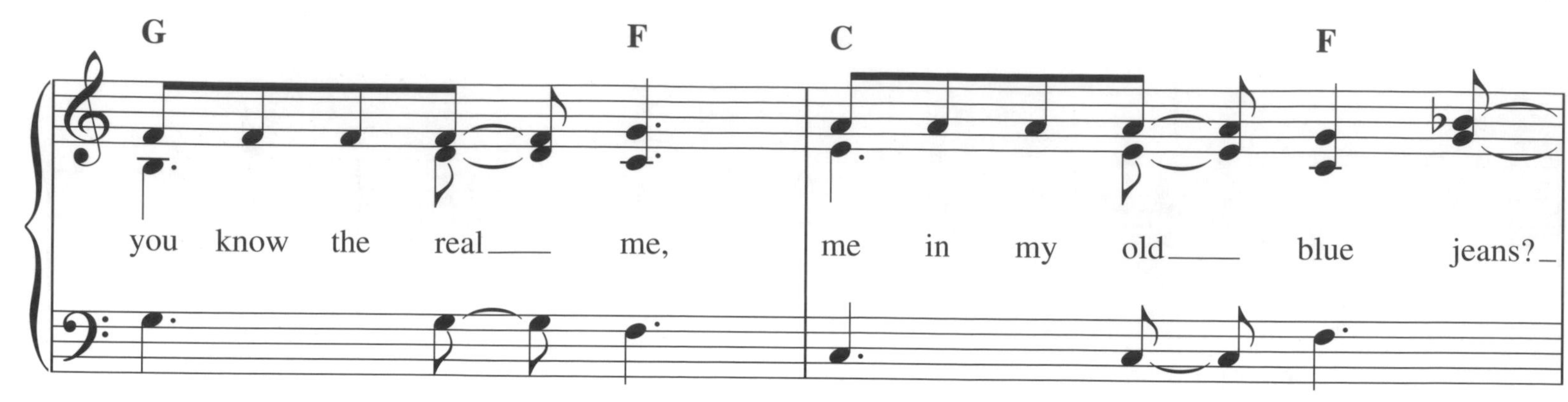
G
F
C
F
you know the real me,
me in my old blue jeans?

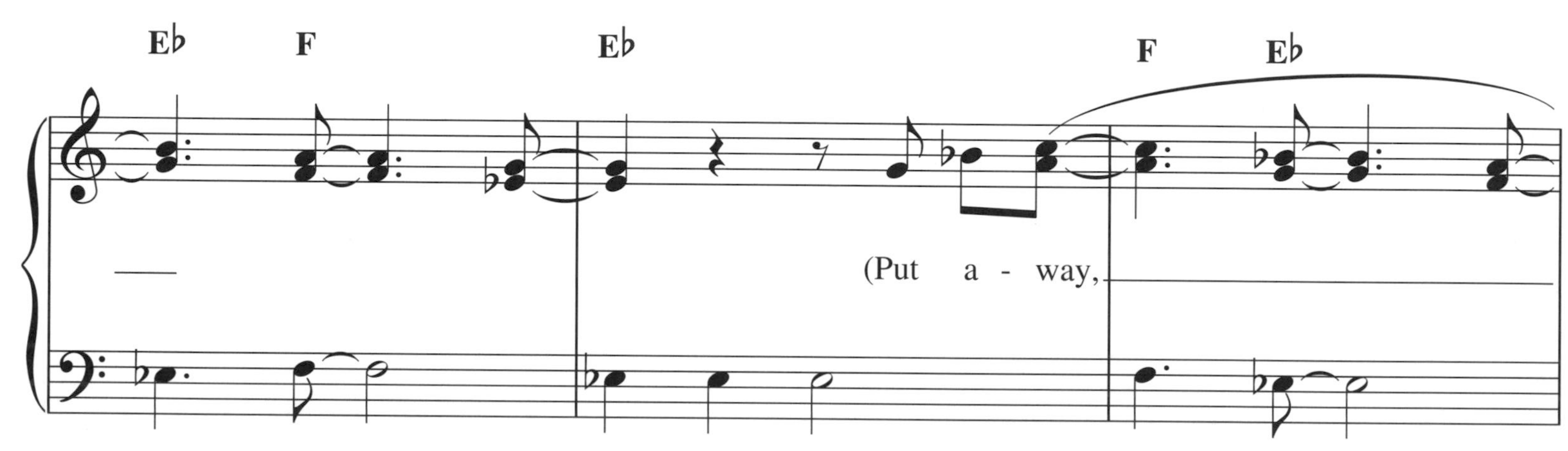
E♭
F
E♭
F
E♭
(Put a - way,

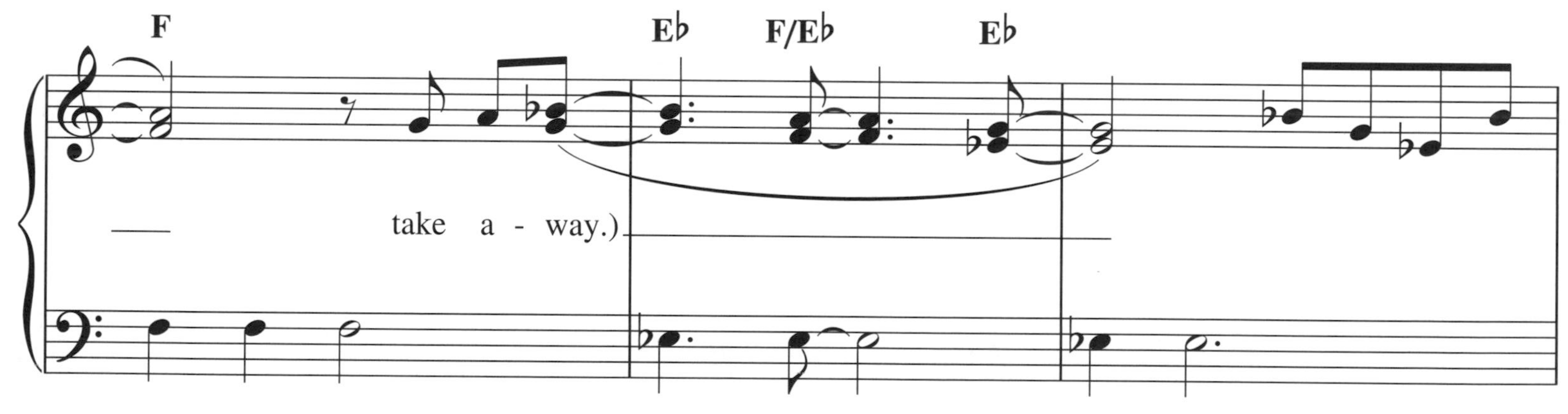
F
E♭
F/E♭
E♭
take a - way.)

D
I wan - na show you what you get. I'm gon - na

G
F
C
F
G
F
put on my old blue jeans,
gon - na
walk out of here in - to

C
F
G
F
the street.
Would you
put up re - sist - ance? Would

C
F
G
F
it make a dif - f'rence? Would
you know the real me,

1., 2.
C
F
3.
C
F
G5
me in my old?... I'm gon - na
me in my old blue jeans?

LIFE'S WHAT YOU MAKE IT

Words and Music by MATTHEW GERRARD
and ROBBIE NEVIL

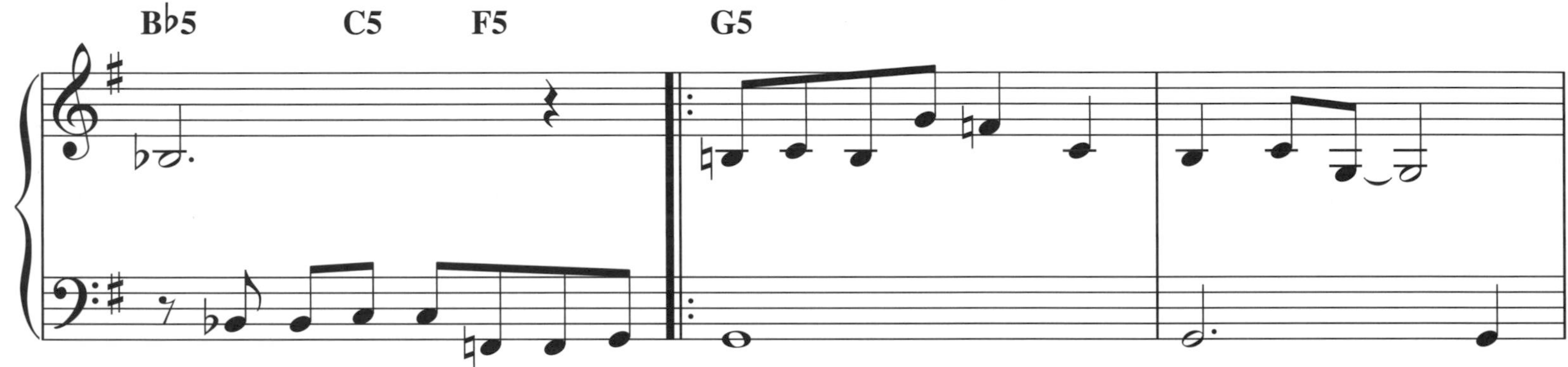

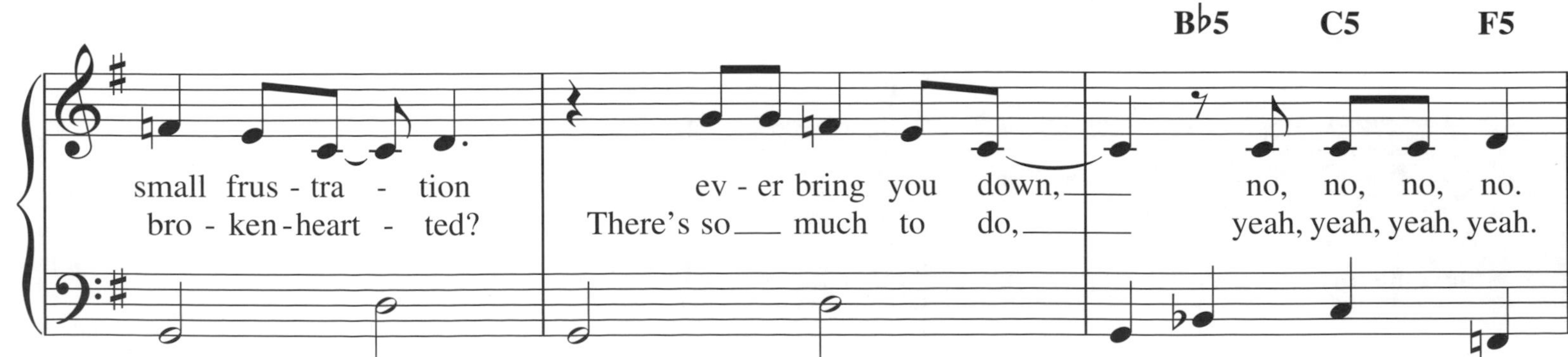

G5
Just take a sit - u - a - tion and turn it all a - round.
Life is hard, or it's a par - ty; the choice is up to you.

B♭5 C5 B♭ C/B♭ B♭ B♭sus2
With a new at - ti - tude, ev - 'ry - thing can change;

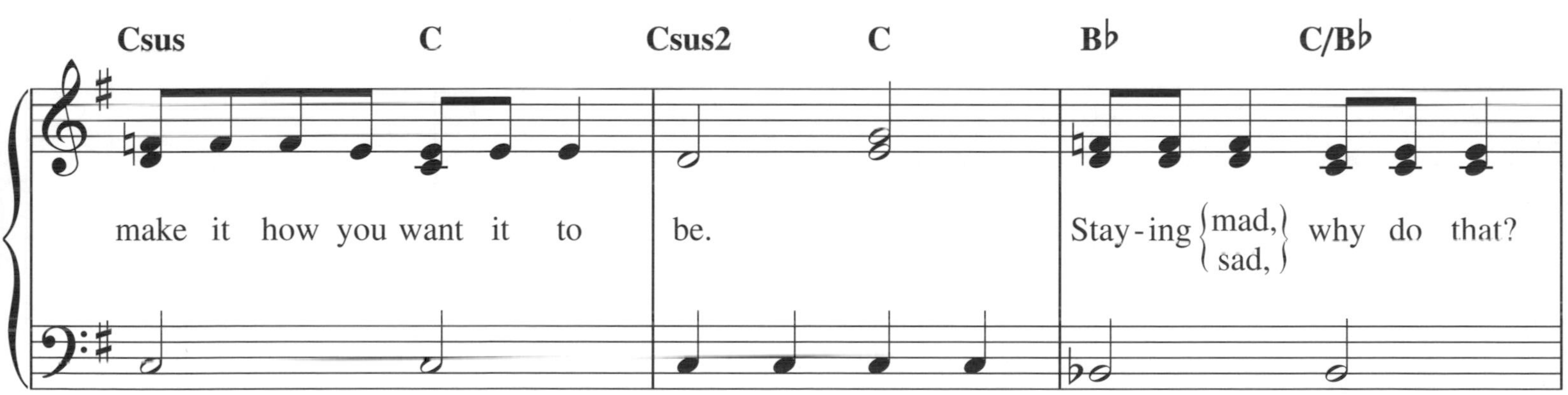
Csus C Csus2 C B♭ C/B♭
make it how you want it to be. Stay - ing {mad, sad,} why do that?

B♭ B♭sus2 Csus C5
Give your - self a break. Laugh a - bout it and you'll see.
I know you wan - na par - ty with me.

G
C
Em
D
Life's what you make it, so let's make it rock.

G
C
Em
D
Life's what you make it, so come on, come on, ev'ry-bod-y now.

G
C
Em
D
Let's cel - e - brate it; join in, ev - 'ry - one. You de-cide,

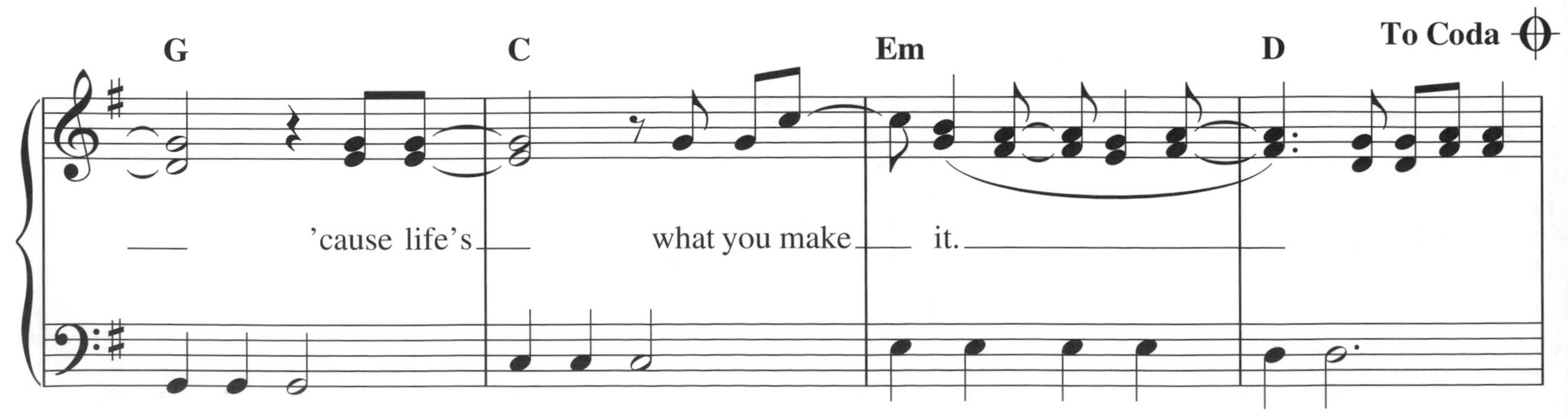
G
C
Em
D
To Coda
'cause life's what you make it.

F
C/E
E♭
Things are look - in' up,
an - y time you want.
All you got - ta do is

B♭/D
F
C/E
re - al - ize that
it's un - der your con - trol,
so let the good times

E♭
B♭5 C5
F5 G5 B♭5 C5
F5 G5
rock and roll.
(Spoken:) Come on, everybody!

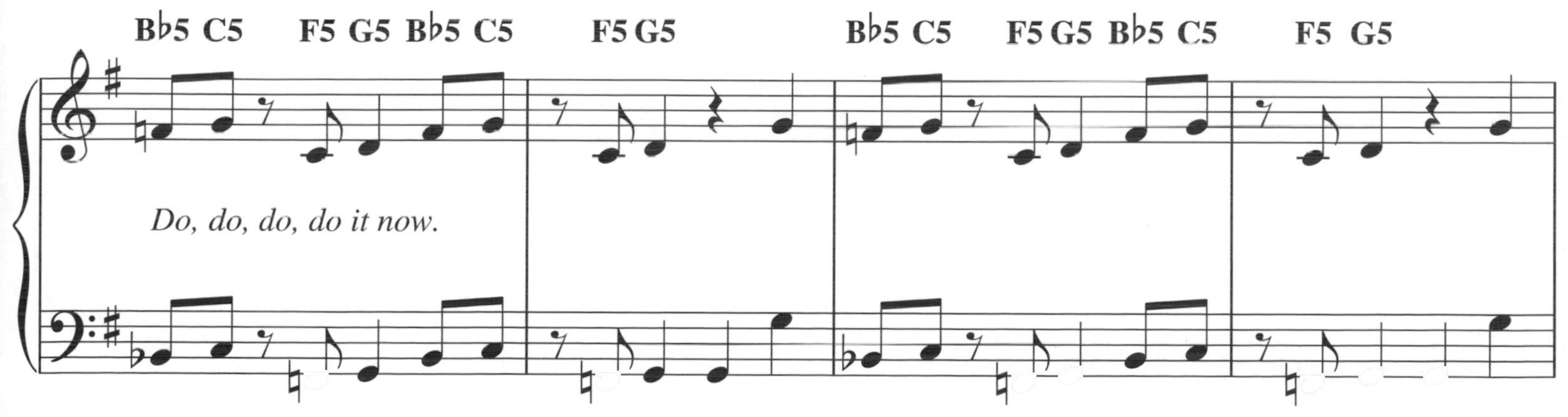
B♭5 C5
F5 G5 B♭5 C5
F5 G5
B♭5 C5
F5 G5 B♭5 C5
F5 G5
Do, do, do, do it now.

D
G5
Ah, ow!
All right! Let's get the

B♭5
C5
F5
party started.

G5
Yeah, yeah, yeah. Now that's a party! Yeah, yeah.

D
D.S. al Coda
(no repeat)
Put your hands together.

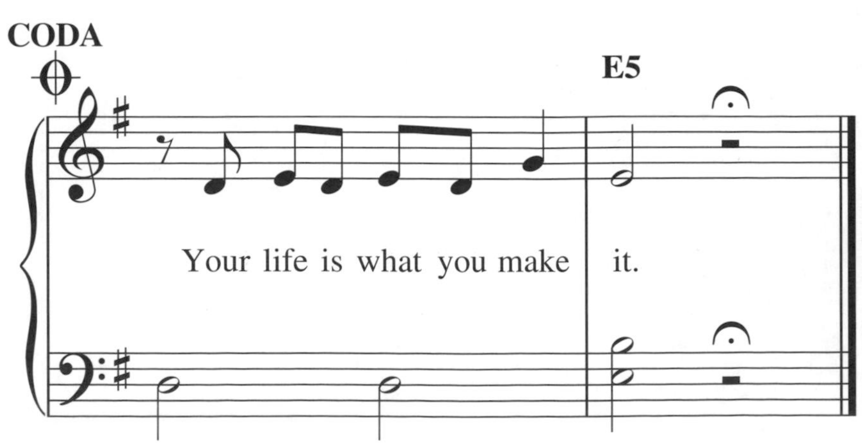
CODA
E5
Your life is what you make it.

ONE IN A MILLION

Words and Music by TOBY GAD
and NEGIN DJAFARI

Moderately, in 2

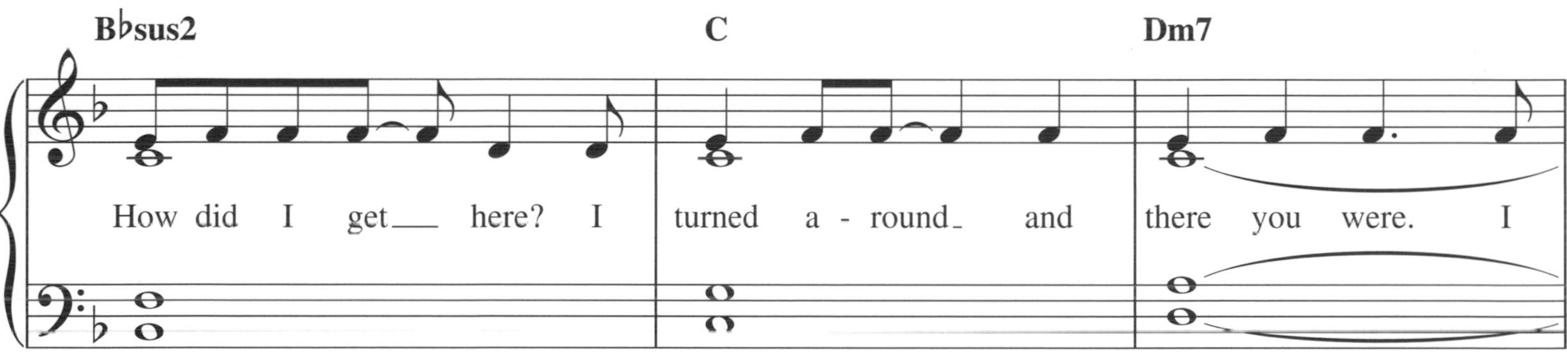

Dm7
Bbsus2
C
that there was more than just chem - is - try. I mean, I

Dm7
Bbsus2
knew you were kind of in - to me, but I fig - ured it's too

C
Dm7
Gm7
good to be true. I said, "Pinch me, where's the

F/A
Bb
F/A
Gm7
catch this time? Can't find a sin - gle cloud in the sky. Help me be - fore I get

F/A
B♭maj9
B♭
used to this guy."
They say that good

F
C
Csus
C
B♭
things take time.
But real - ly great

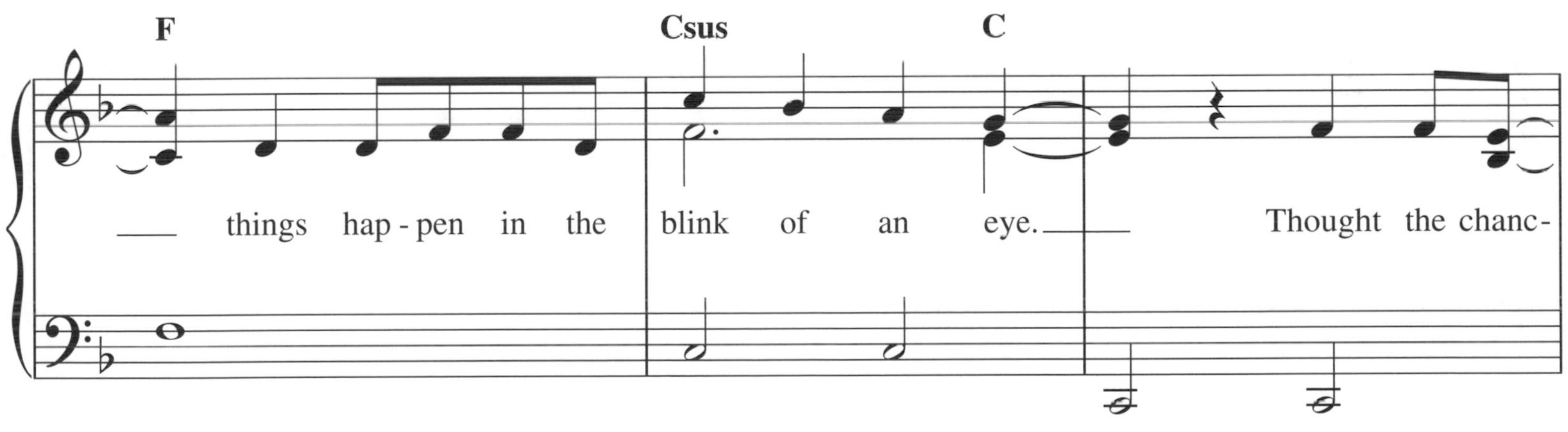
F
Csus
C
things hap - pen in the blink of an eye.
Thought the chanc -

Gm7
Dm7
B♭
- es to meet some - bod - y like you were a mil - lion to one.

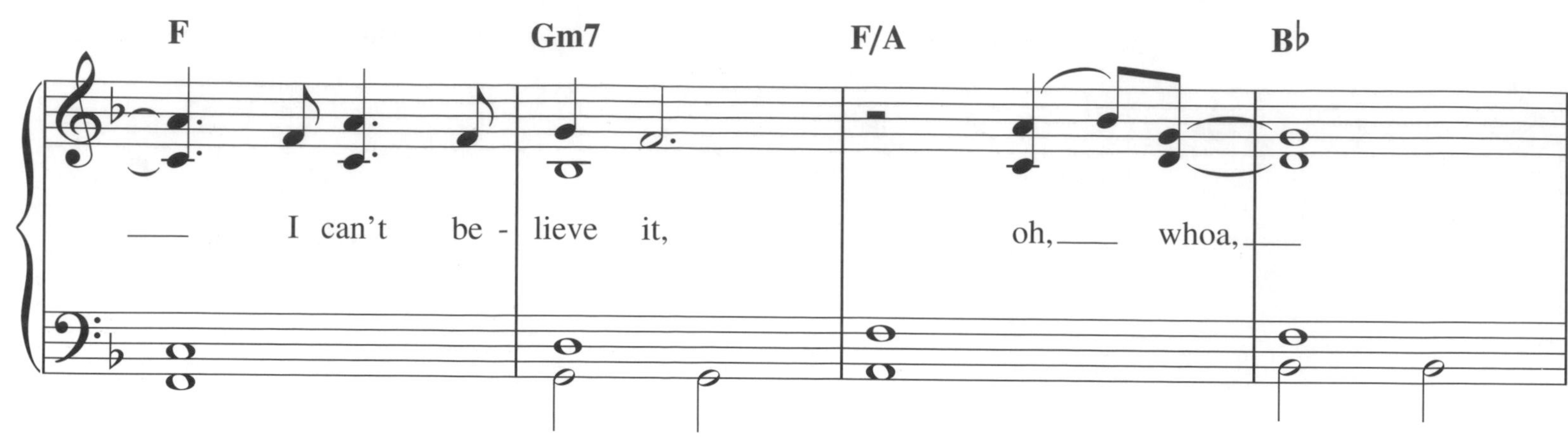
F
Gm7
F/A
B♭
I can't be - lieve it,
oh, whoa,

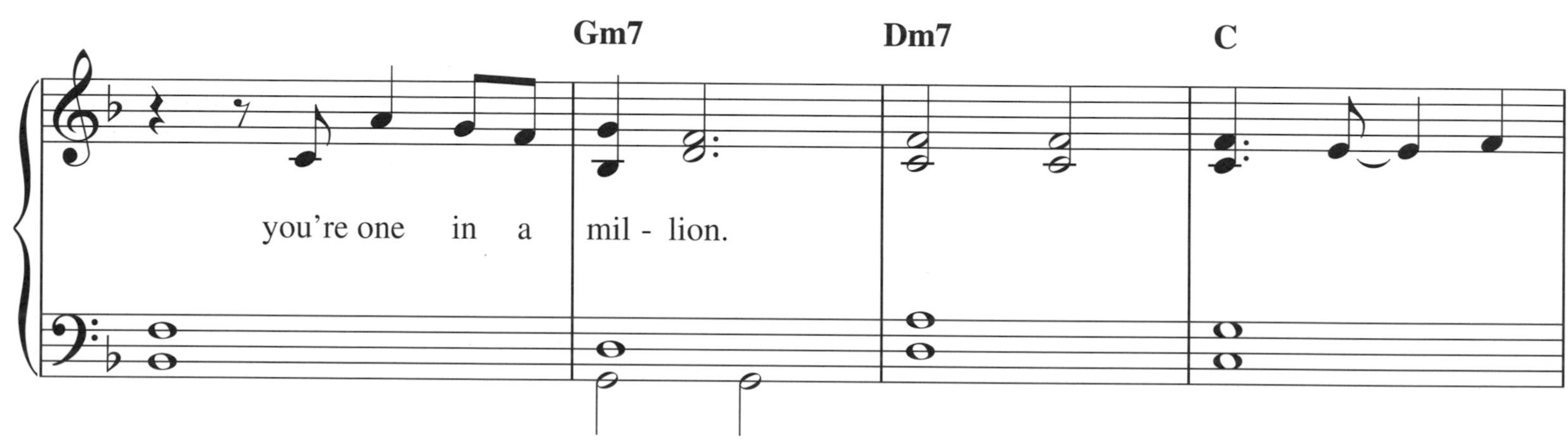
Gm7
Dm7
C
you're one in a mil - lion.

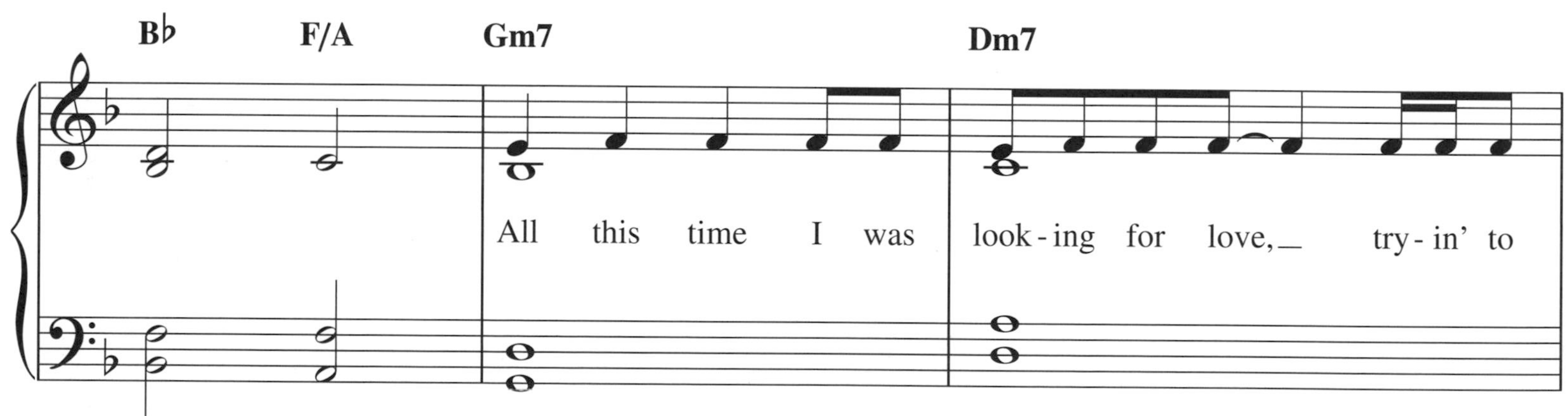
B♭
F/A
Gm7
Dm7
All this time I was look - ing for love, try - in' to

B♭sus2
Csus
Gm7
F/A
make things work that weren't good e - nough, 'til I thought I'm through,

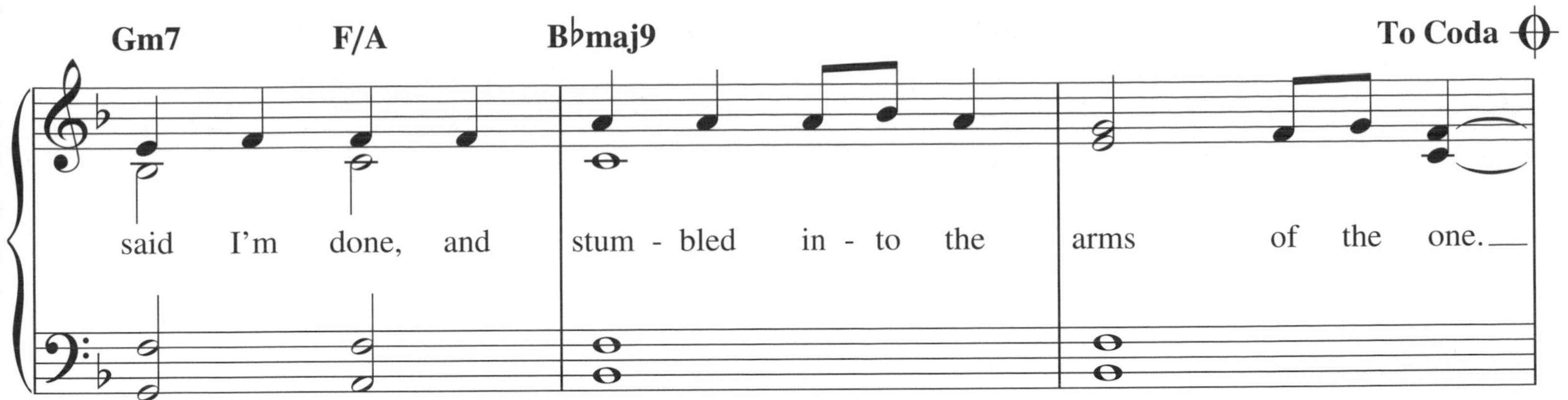
Gm7
F/A
B♭maj9
To Coda
said I'm done, and stum - bled in - to the arms of the one.

B♭sus2
You're mak - in' me laugh a - bout the

C
Dm7
sil - li - est stuff, say that I'm your dia - mond in the rough. When I'm mad

B♭sus2
C
Dm7
at you, you come with your vel - vet touch. Can't be -

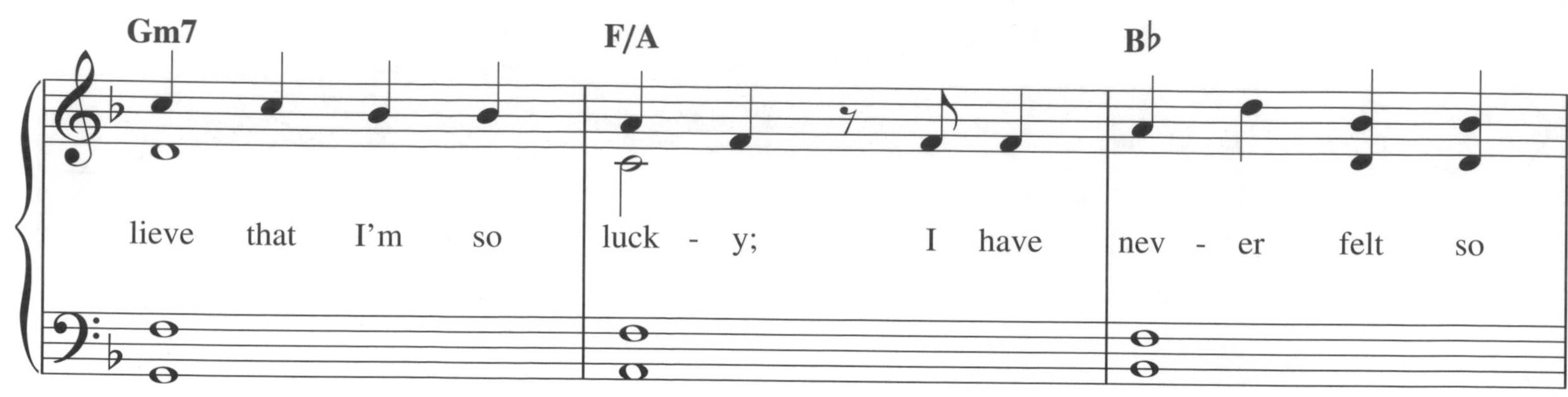
Gm7
F/A
B♭
lieve that I'm so luck - y; I have nev - er felt so

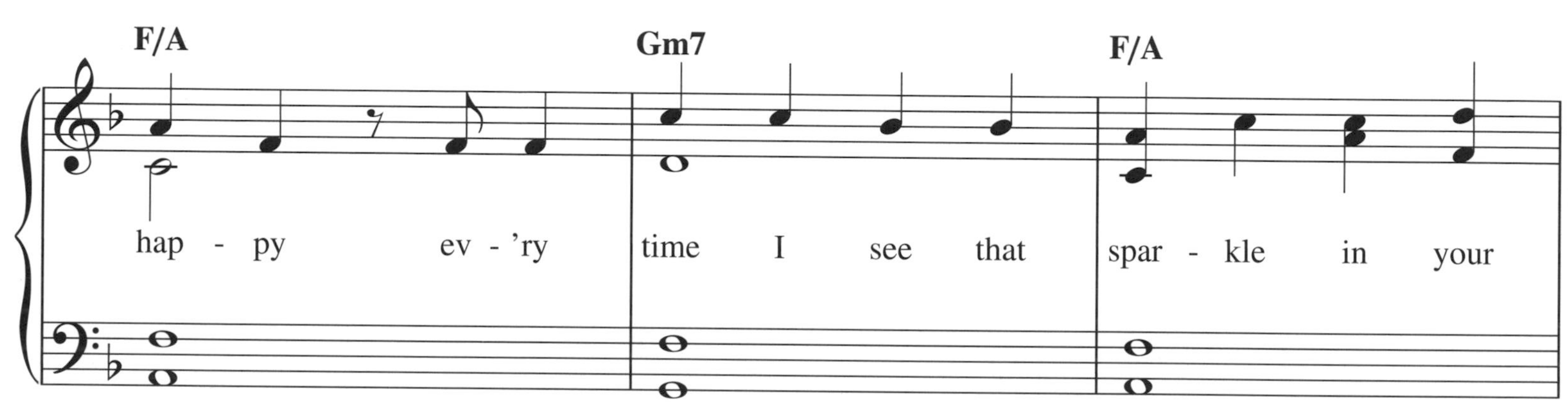
F/A
Gm7
F/A
hap - py ev - 'ry time I see that spar - kle in your

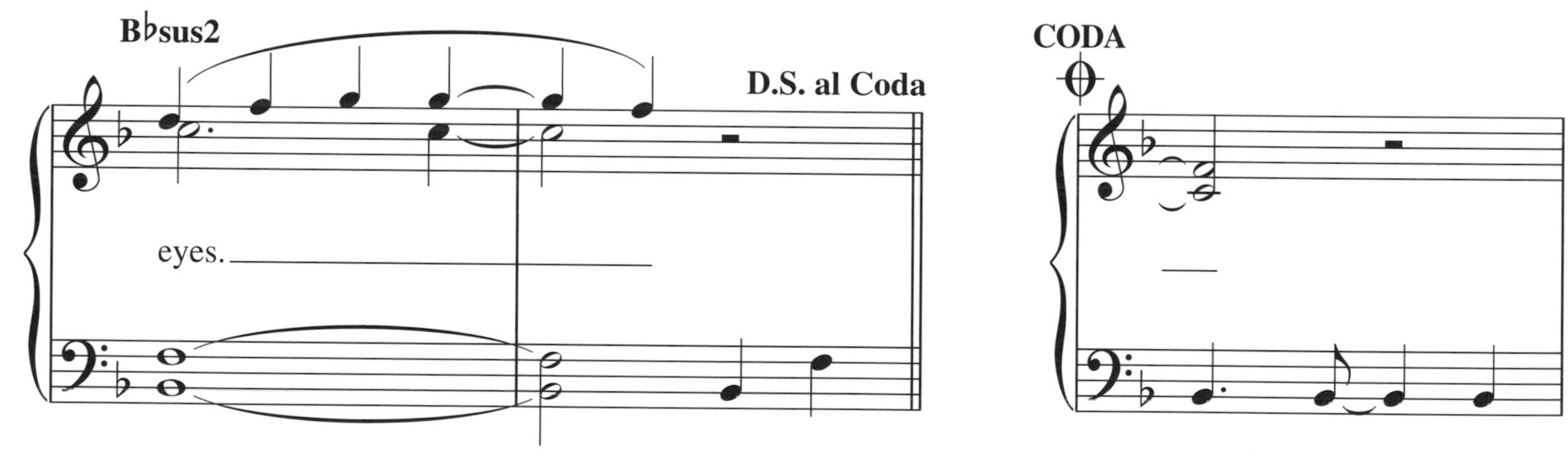
B♭sus2
D.S. al Coda
CODA
eyes.

Gm7
I said, "Pinch me, where's the

F/A
B♭
F/A
catch this time?
Can't find a sin - gle
cloud in the sky.

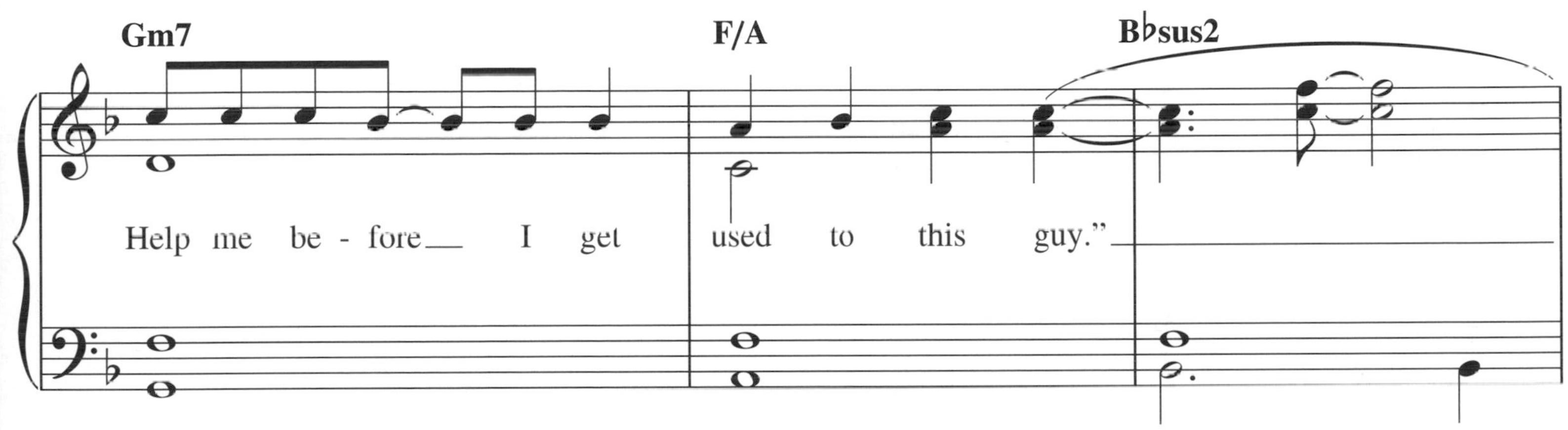
Gm7
F/A
B♭sus2
Help me be - fore I get
used to this guy."

B♭
F
They say that good
things take time.

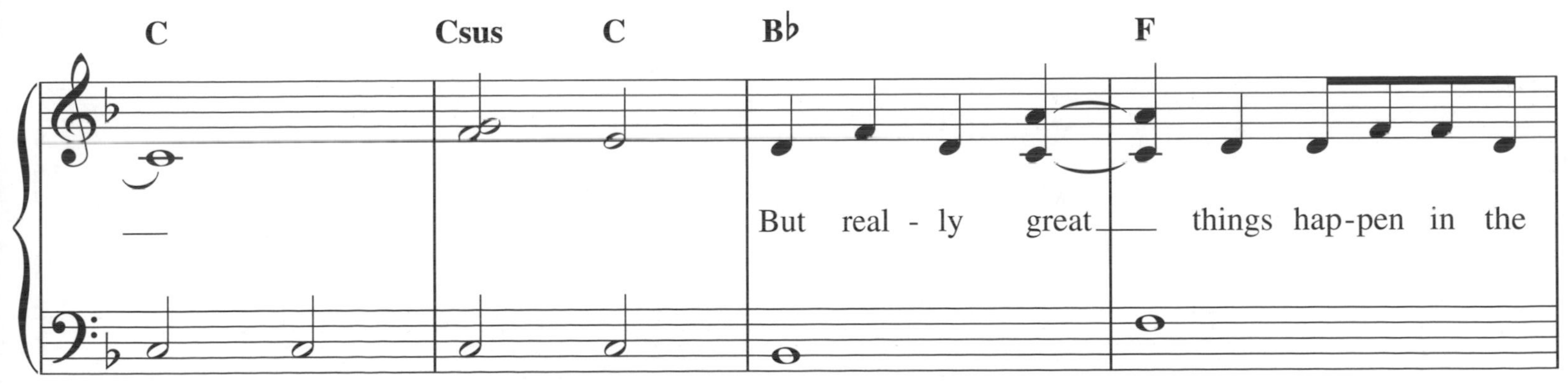
C
Csus
C
B♭
F
But real - ly great
things hap-pen in the

Csus
C
Gm7
blink of an eye.
Thought the chanc - es to meet some - bod -

Dm7
Bb
F
- y like you were a mil - lion to one.
I can't be -

Gm7
1.
F/A
Bbmaj9
lieve it,
oh, whoa,
yeah, yeah.

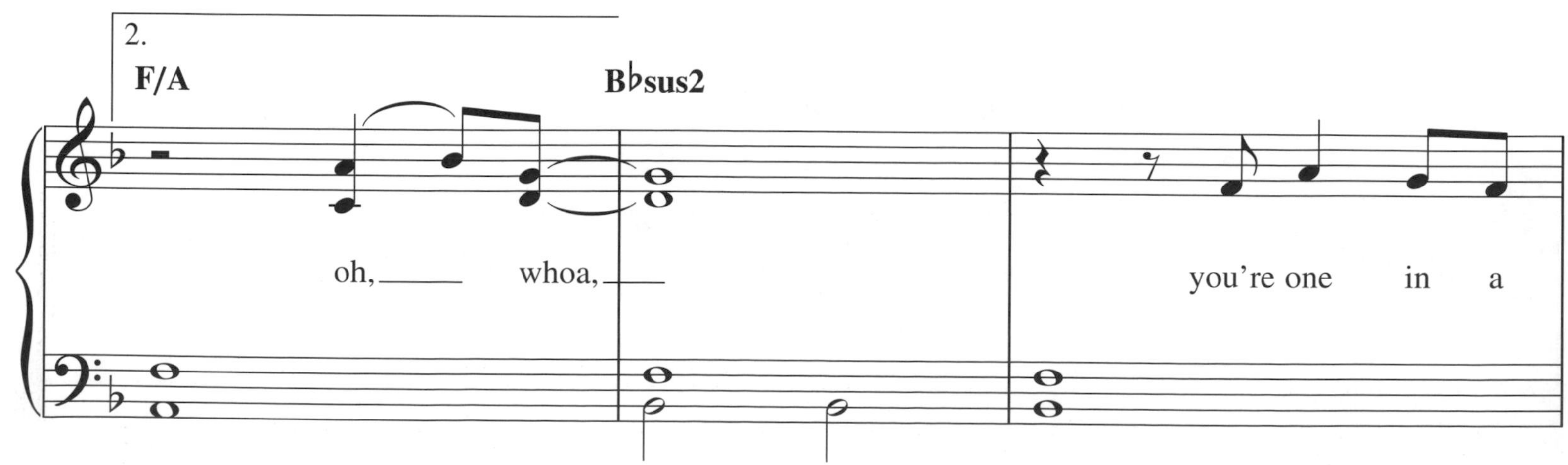
2.
F/A
Bbsus2
oh, whoa,
you're one in a

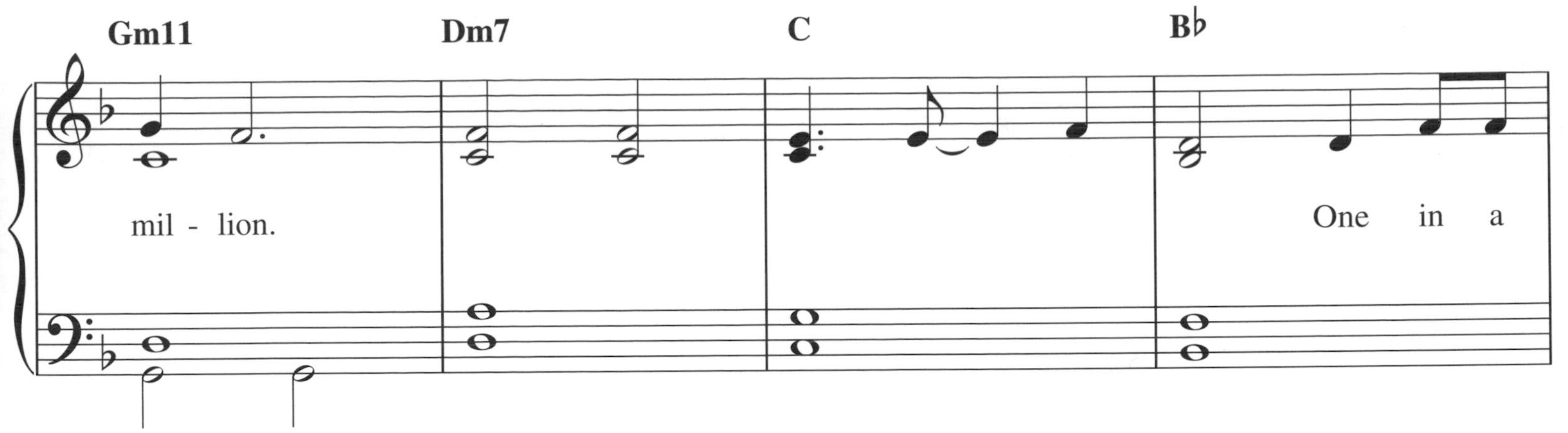
Gm11
Dm7
C
B♭
mil - lion.
One in a

Gm11
Dm7
F
C
mil - lion.
You're one in a

Gm7
F/A
B♭sus2
mil - lion.

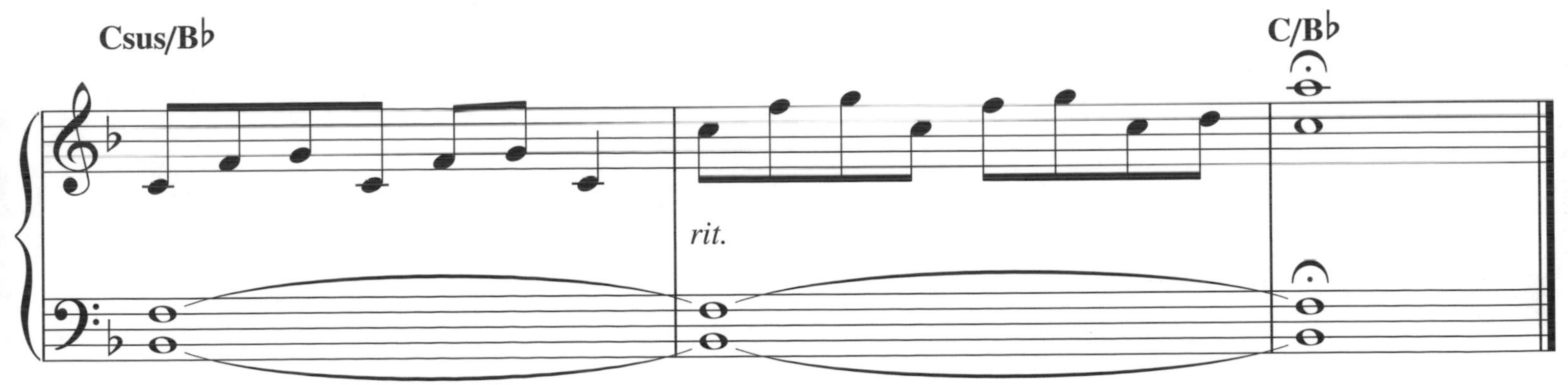
Csus/B♭
C/B♭
rit.

BIGGER THAN US

Words and Music by TIM JAMES
and ANTONINA ARMATO

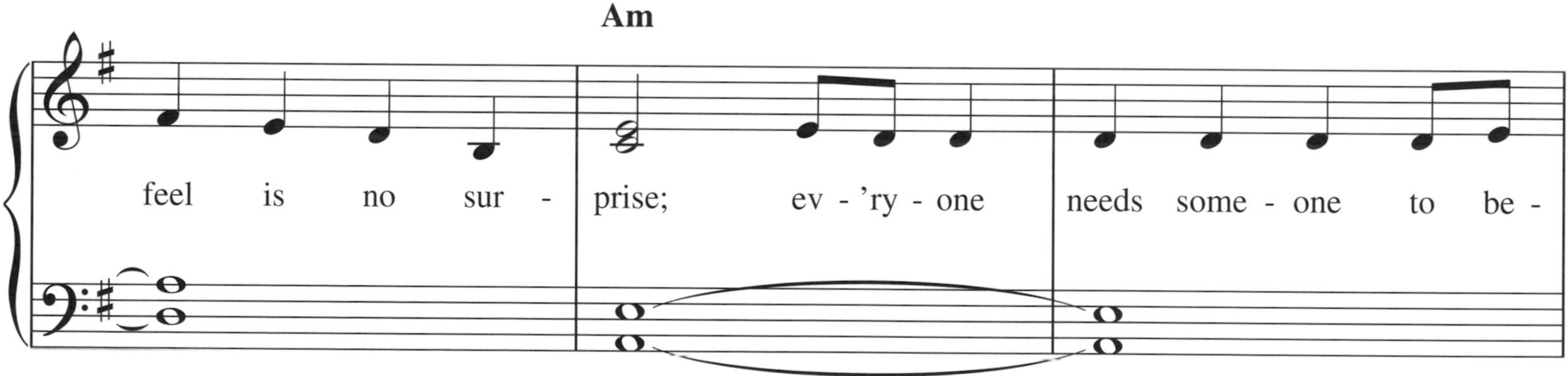

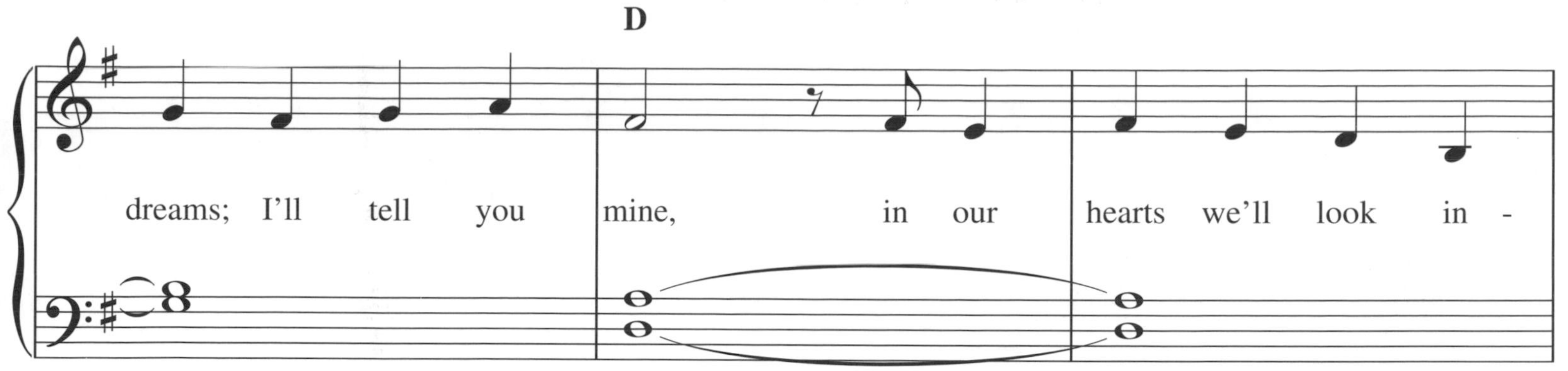
D
dreams; I'll tell you mine, in our hearts we'll look in -

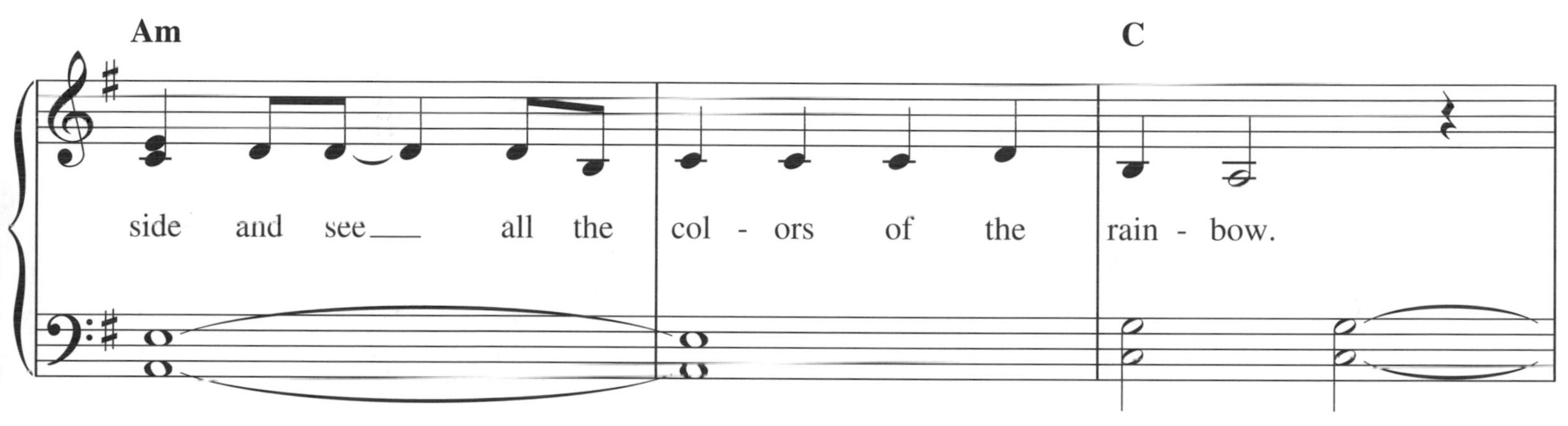
Am
C
side and see all the col - ors of the rain - bow.

G
I know. We all want to be - lieve in love.

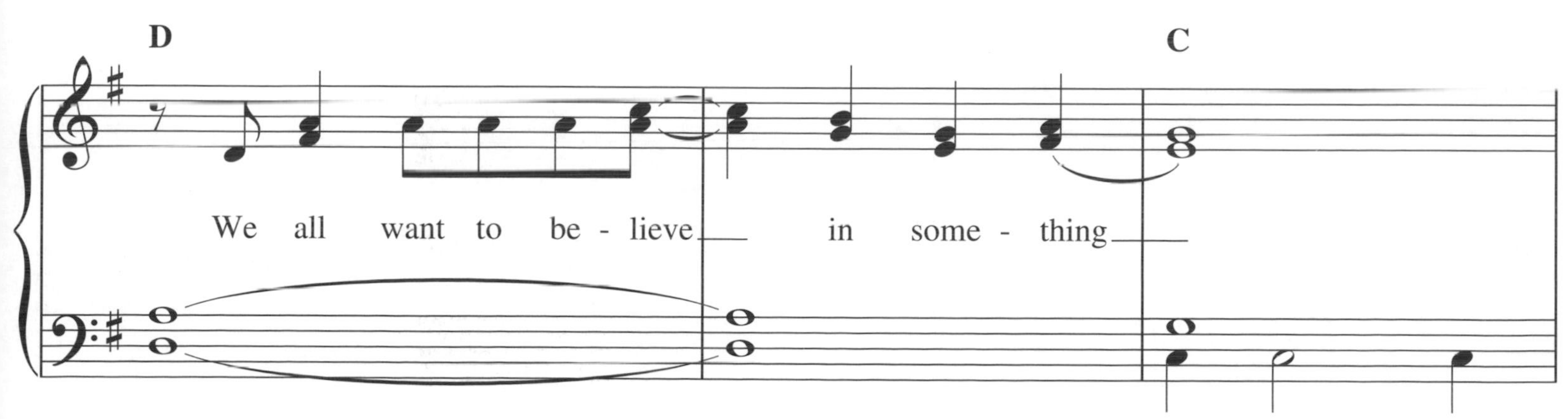
D
C
We all want to be - lieve in some - thing

G
D
G
big - ger than just us.
We all want to

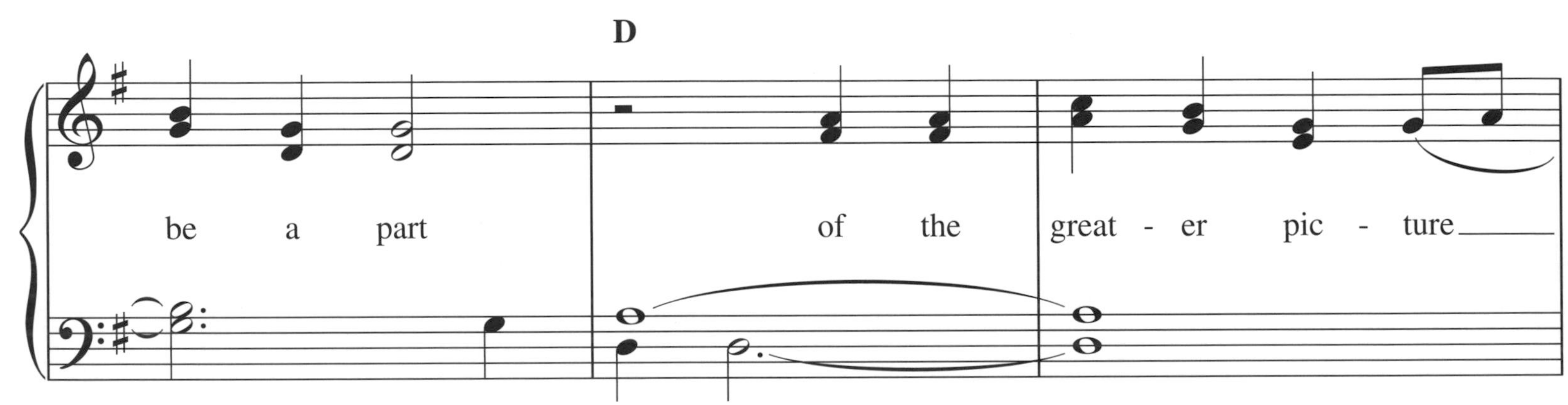
D
be a part
of the
great - er pic - ture

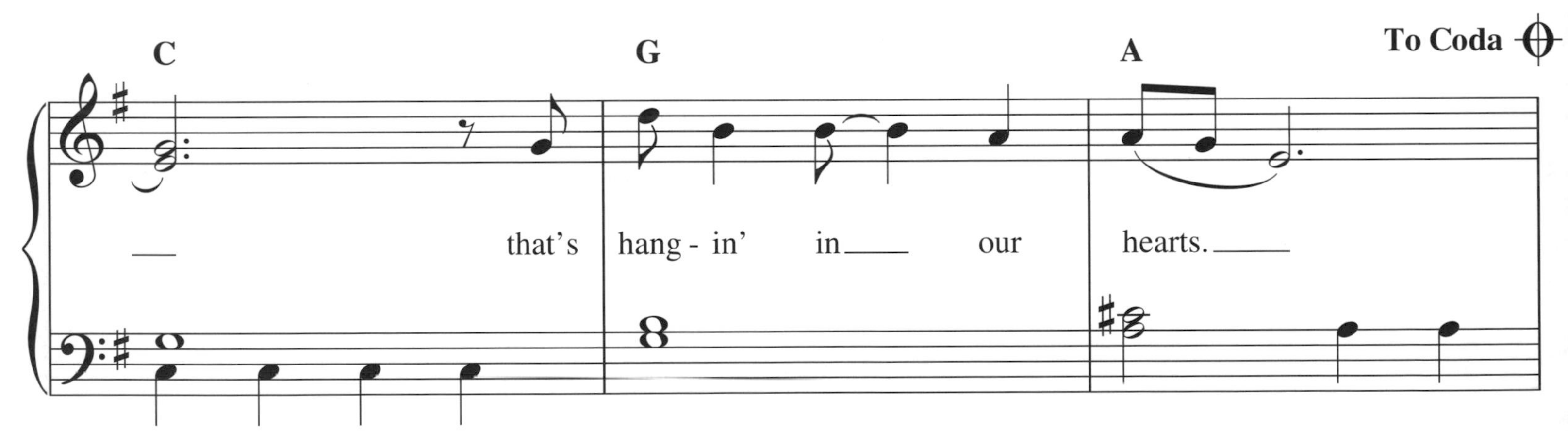
C
G
A
To Coda
that's
hang - in' in our
hearts.

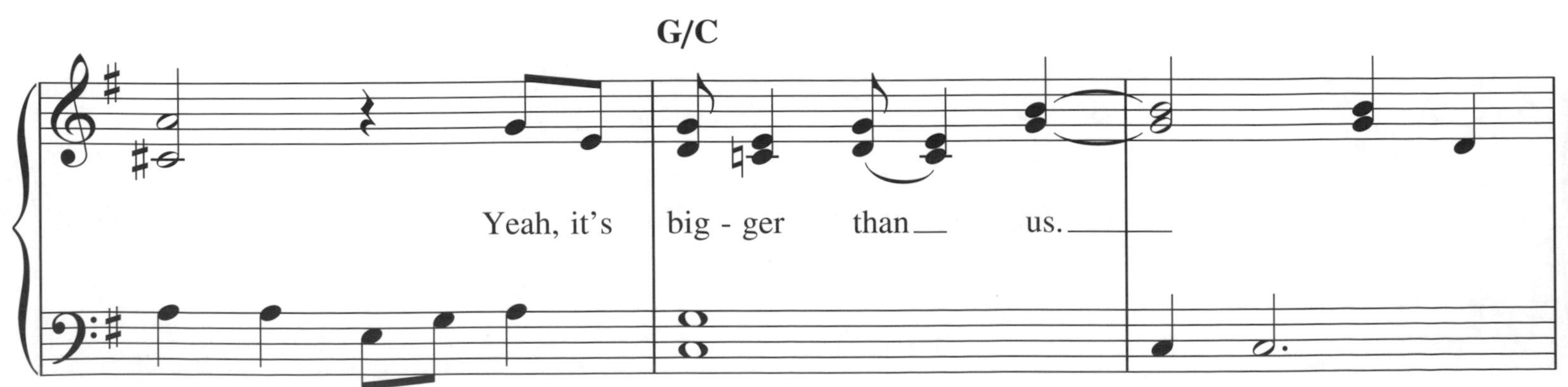
G/C
Yeah, it's
big - ger than us.

G
D
I want to see be - yond my own lit - tle world, grab your hand

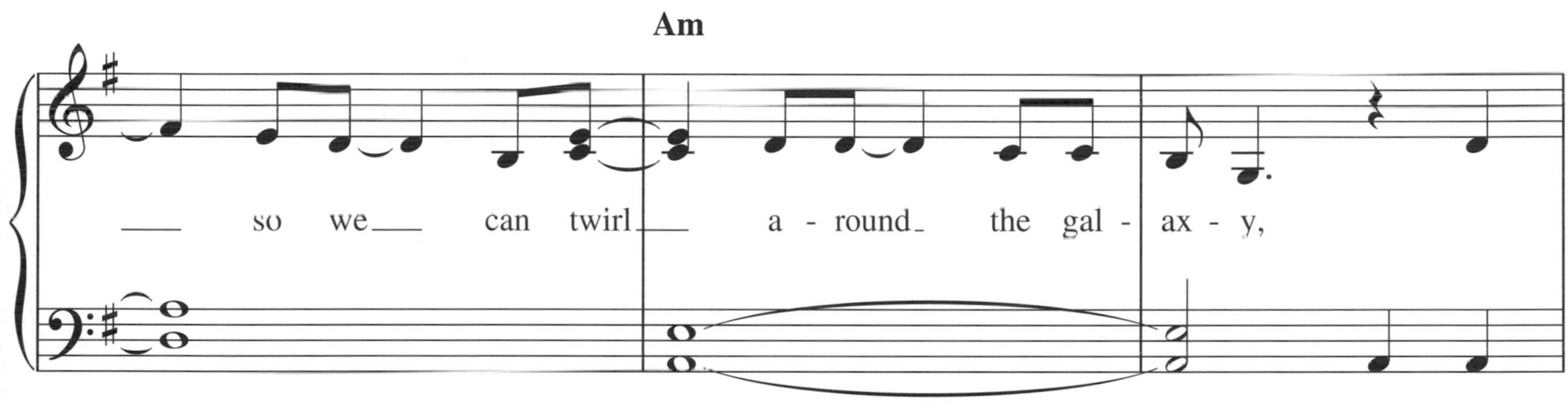
Am
so we can twirl a - round the gal - ax - y,

C
G
see the world with clar - i - ty, oh, whoa. Oh, whoa,

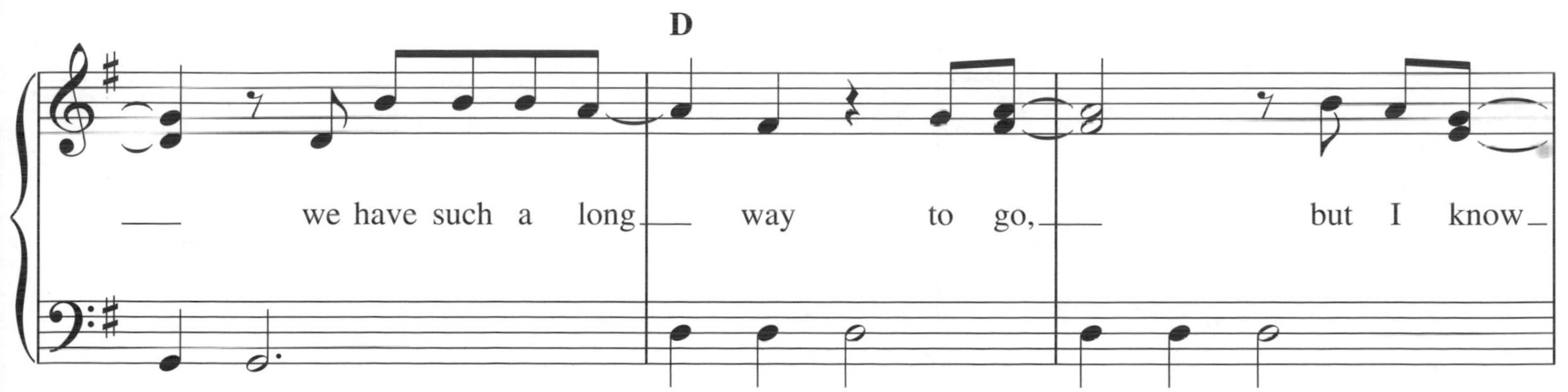
D
we have such a long way to go, but I know

Am
G/C
we're get-ting clos - er ev - 'ry day, ev - 'ry day.

D.S. al Coda

CODA
A7
Yeah, it's big-ger than us,

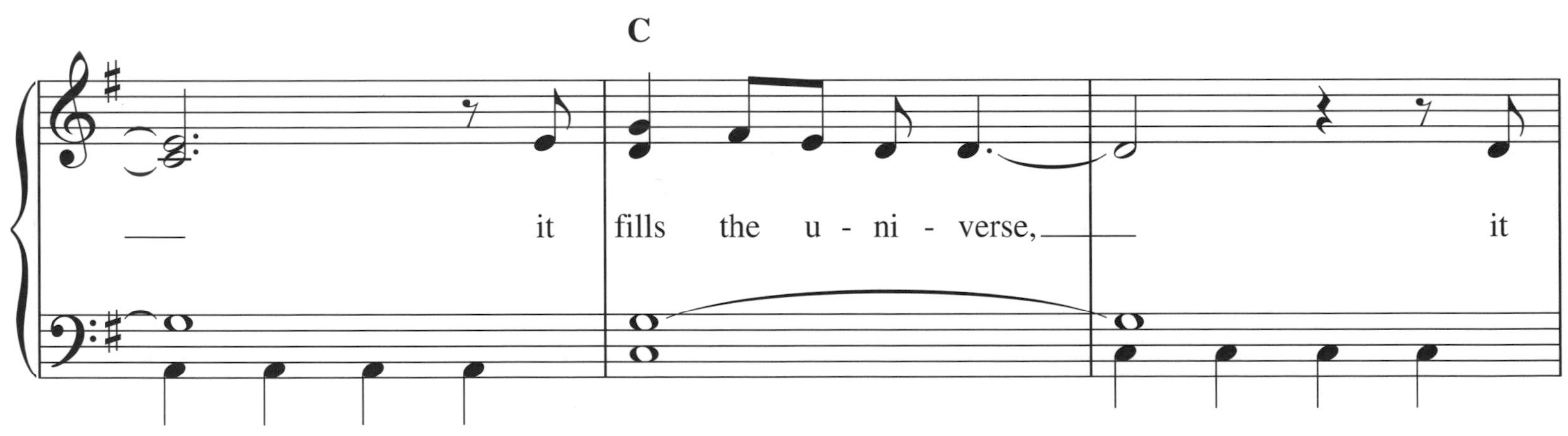
C
it fills the u - ni - verse, it

A7
C
lights the skies a - bove and res - cues all our

G
hearts with love, (L - O - V - E, love.) with

D
C
love. (L - O - V - E, love.)

G
A
That's what's big - ger than us.

G/C
Em7
It's love, it's love that's big - ger than us. It's love, it's

D
love that's big - ger than us.
It's love, it's
love.

G
We all want to be - lieve

D
in love.
We all want to be - lieve
in some - thing

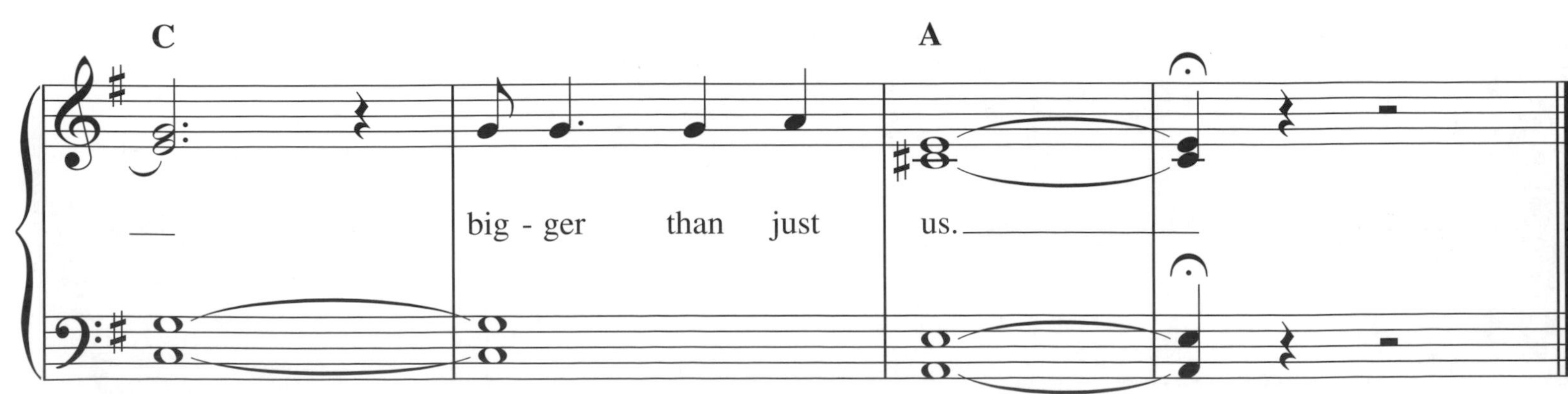
C
A
big - ger than just
us.

YOU AND ME TOGETHER

Words and Music by
JAMIE HOUSTON

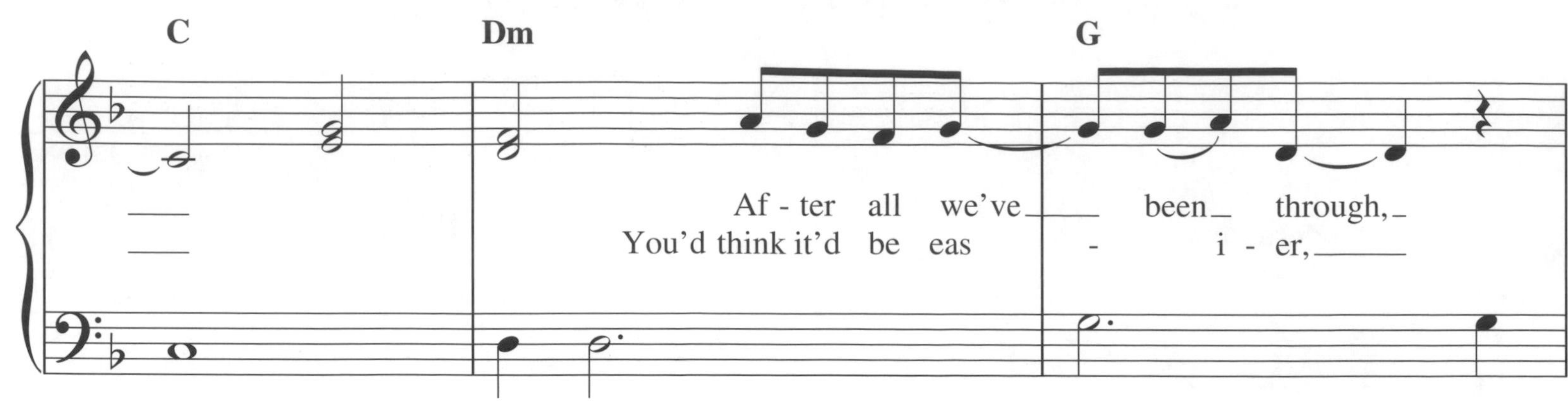
C
Dm
G
Af - ter all we've been through,
You'd think it'd be eas - i - er,

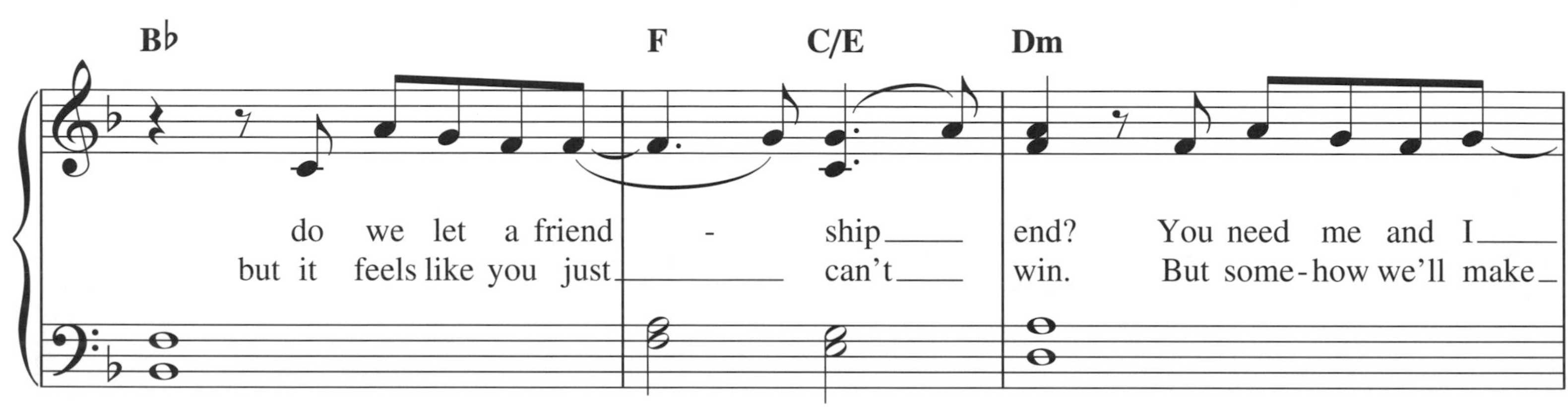
B♭
F
C/E
Dm
do we let a friend - ship end? You need me and I
but it feels like you just can't win. But some-how we'll make

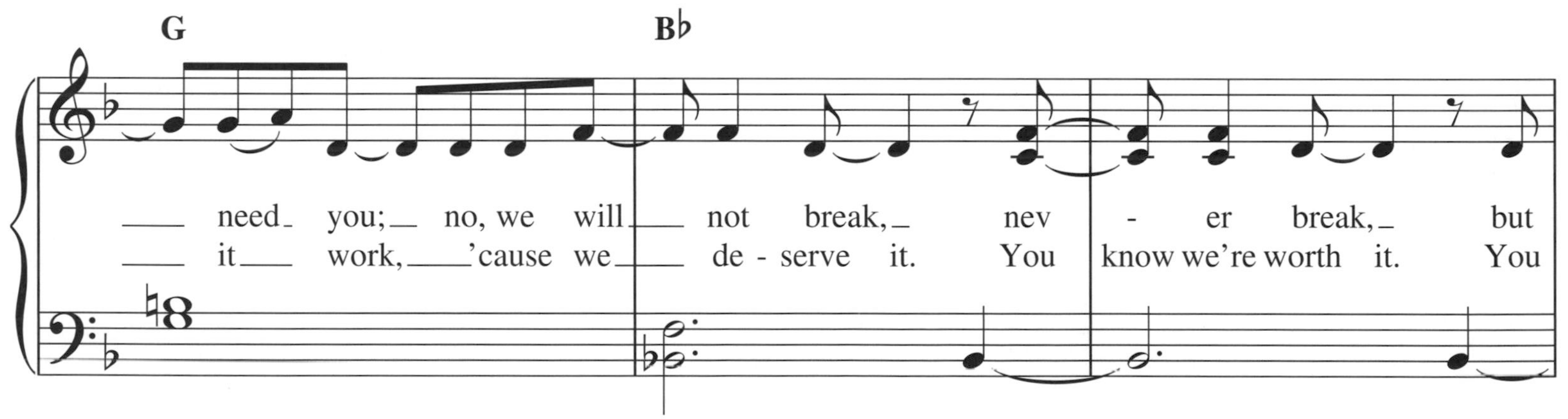
G
B♭
need you; no, we will not break, nev - er break, but
it work, 'cause we de - serve it. You know we're worth it. You

F
e - ven if we bend, yeah,
can't give up on friends, 'cause
it's you and me

C
B♭maj9
F
to - geth - er.
Yeah, I'm al - ways on

C
B♭maj9
F
your side.
No one, no one, no one

C
Dm7
B♭
can ev - er change it;
come on, let 'em try,
'cause it's you

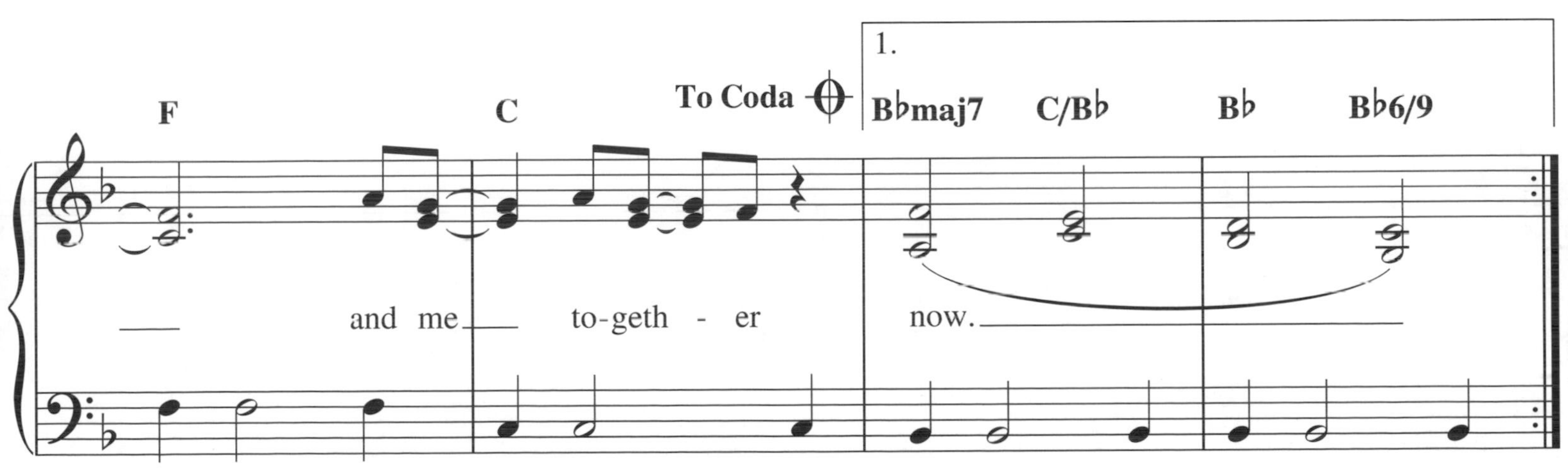
F
C
To Coda
1.
B♭maj7
C/B♭
B♭
B♭6/9
and me to-geth - er
now.

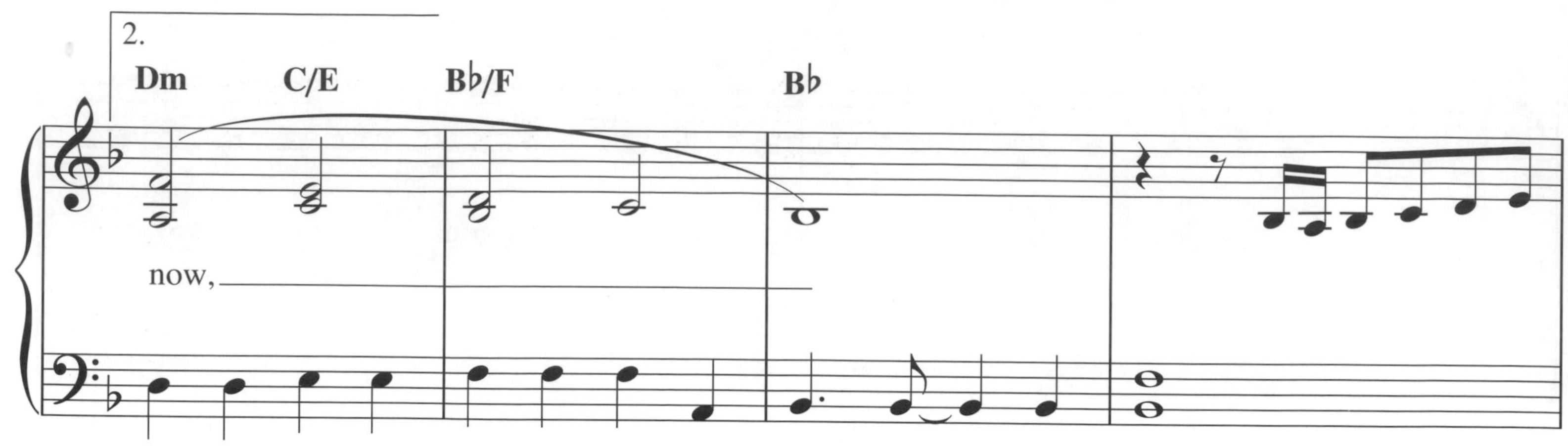
2.
Dm
C/E
B♭/F
B♭
now,

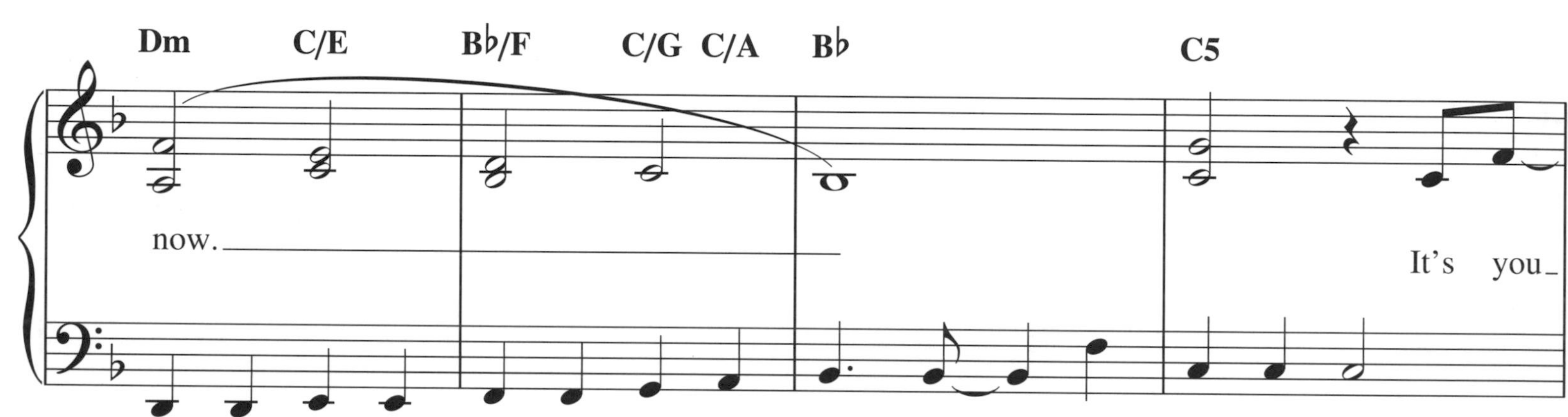
Dm
C/E
B♭/F
C/G
C/A
B♭
C5
now.
It's you

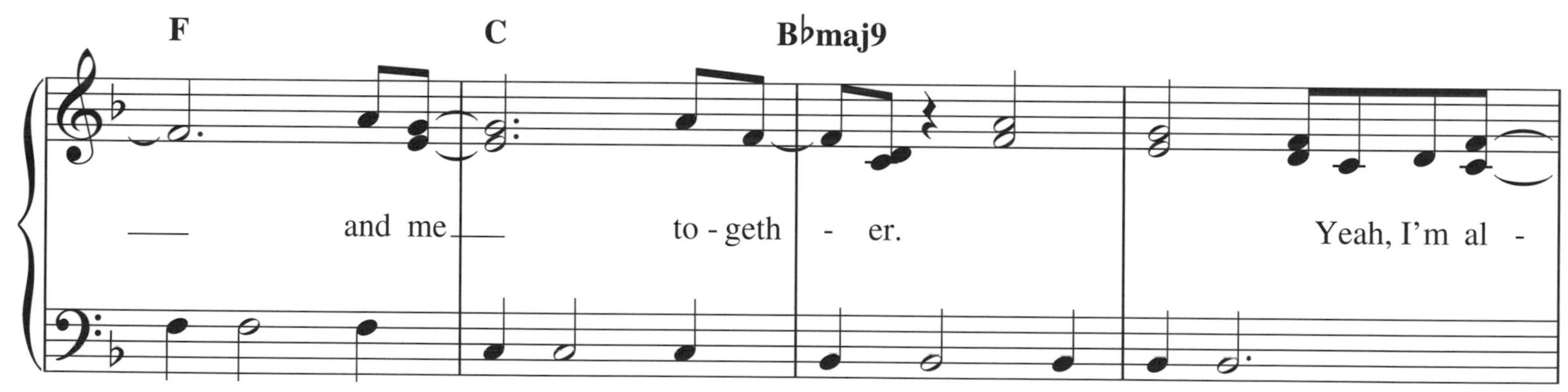
F
C
B♭maj9
and me
to - geth - er.
Yeah, I'm al -

F
C
B♭maj9
- ways on
your side.

F
C
No one, no one, no one can ev - er change it;

Dm7
B♭
come on, let 'em try.
Come on, let 'em try.

D.S. al Coda
It's you

CODA
B♭maj7
C/B♭
now,

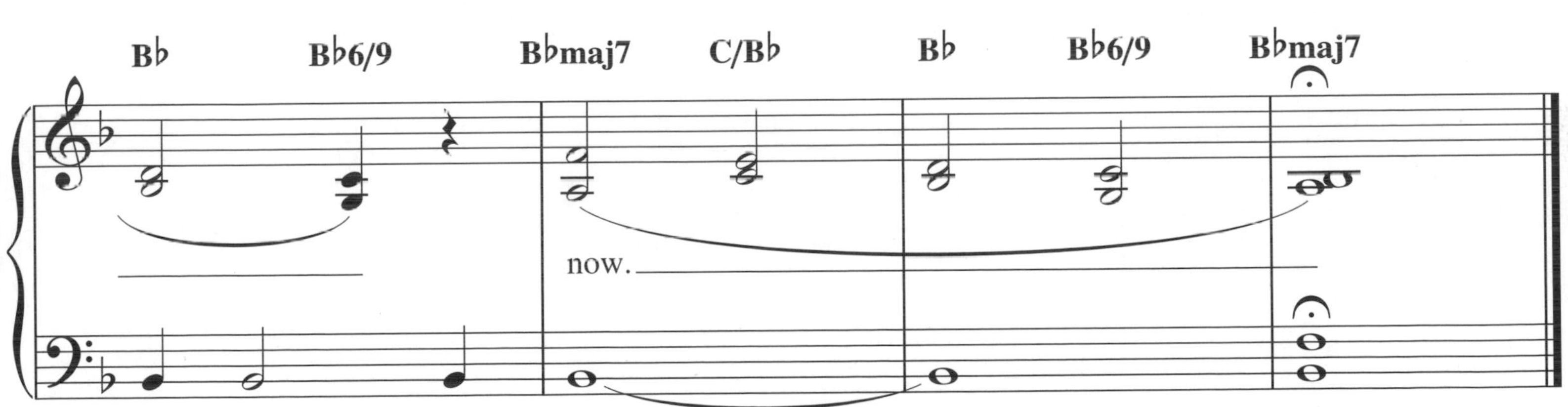
B♭
B♭6/9
B♭maj7
C/B♭
B♭
B♭6/9
B♭maj7
now.

TRUE FRIEND

Words and Music by
JEANNIE LURIE

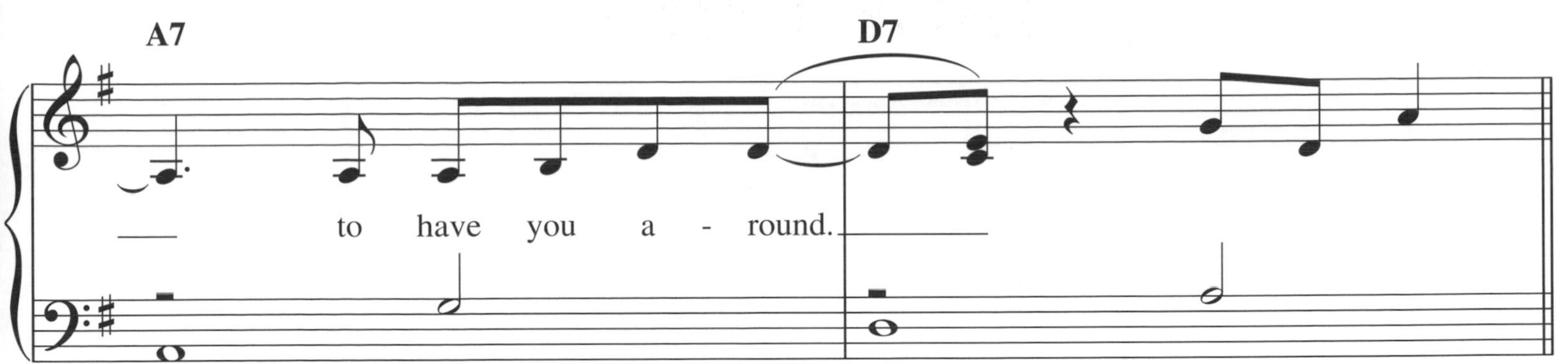
A7
D7
to have you a - round.

G
C
G
You know the se - crets I could nev - er tell,
You don't get an - gry when I change the plans.

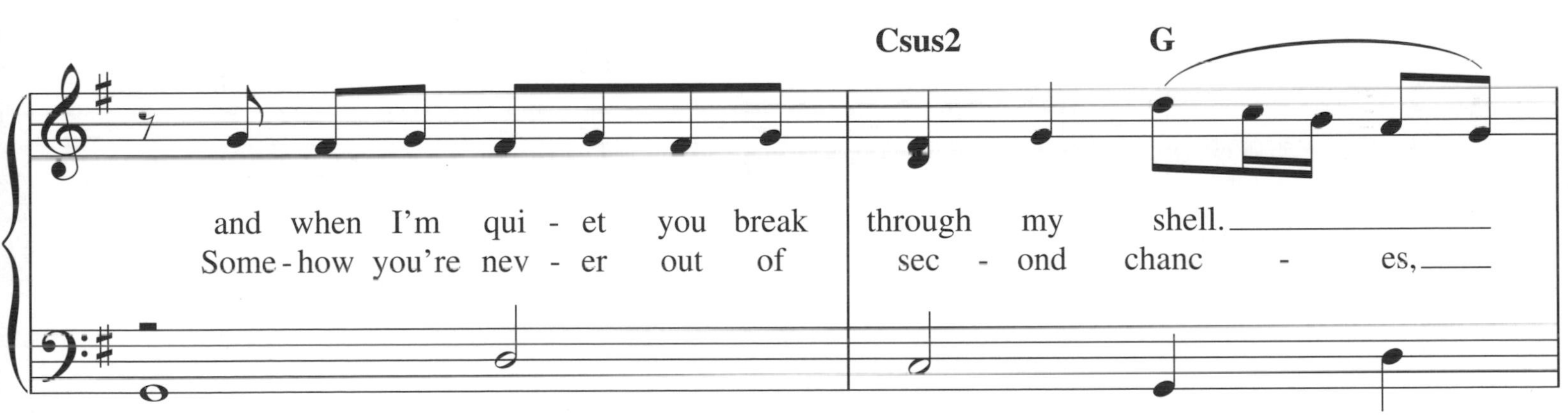
Csus2
G
and when I'm qui - et you break through my shell.
Some - how you're nev - er out of sec - ond chanc - es,

C
G
Don't feel the need to do a re - bel yell, 'cause you keep
won't say "I told you" when I'm wrong a - gain. I'm so luck -

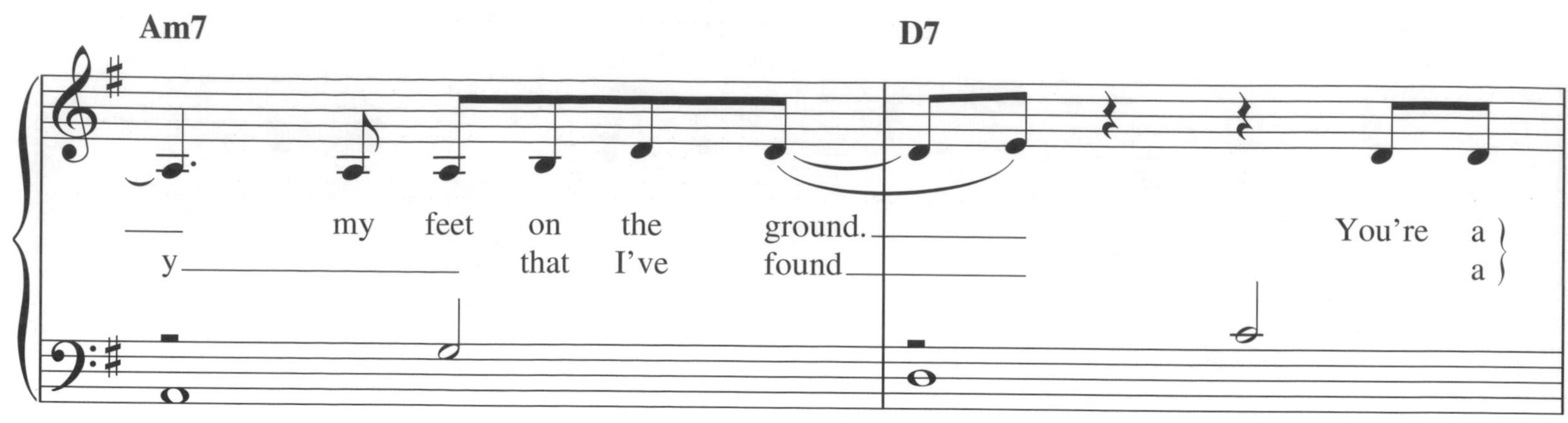
Am7
D7
my feet on the ground.
You're a
y
that I've found
a

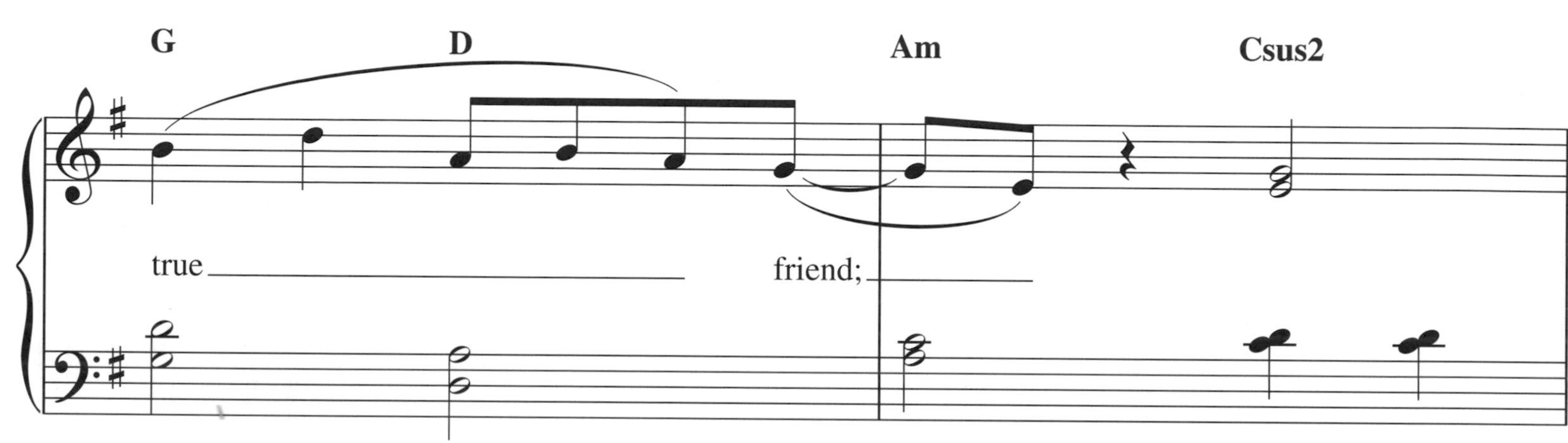
G
D
Am
Csus2
true
friend;

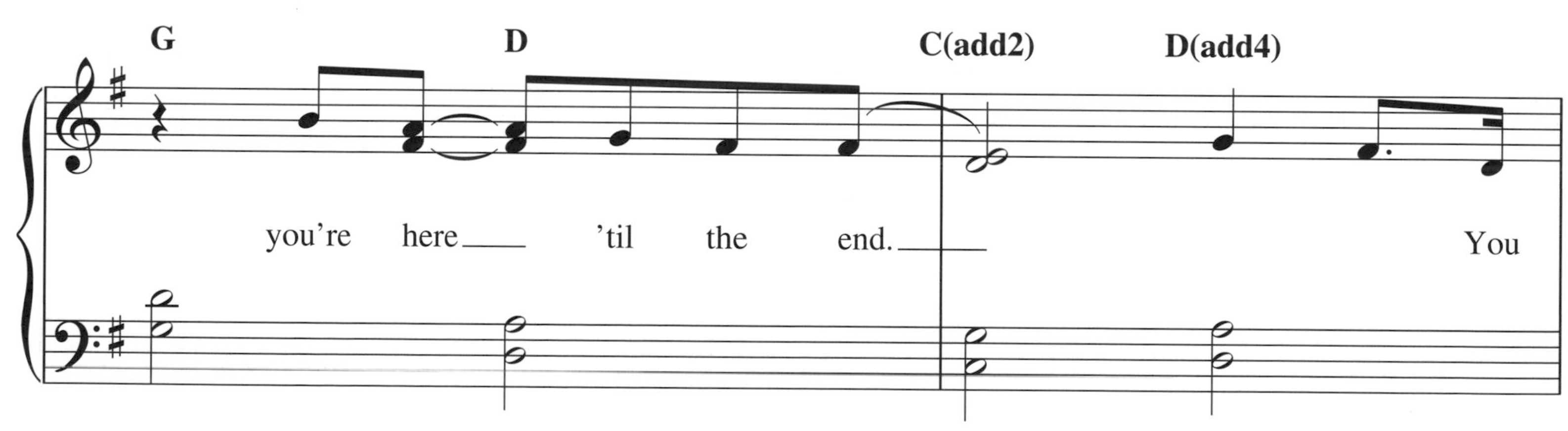
G
D
C(add2)
D(add4)
you're here 'til the end.
You

G
D(add4)
Am
C
pull me a - side when some-thin' ain't right,
talk with me now and in - to the night,

1.
2.
Em7
D
C(add2)
Gsus2
'til it's al-right a - gain.
You're a true friend.
True
B7
Em
friends will go to the ends
A7
of the earth 'til they find the thing you need.
Friends hang on through the ups and the downs, 'cause they've got

A7
C
D
G
D
some - one to be - lieve in. A true friend;

Am7
Csus2
G
D
C(add2)
D(add4)
you're here 'til the end. You

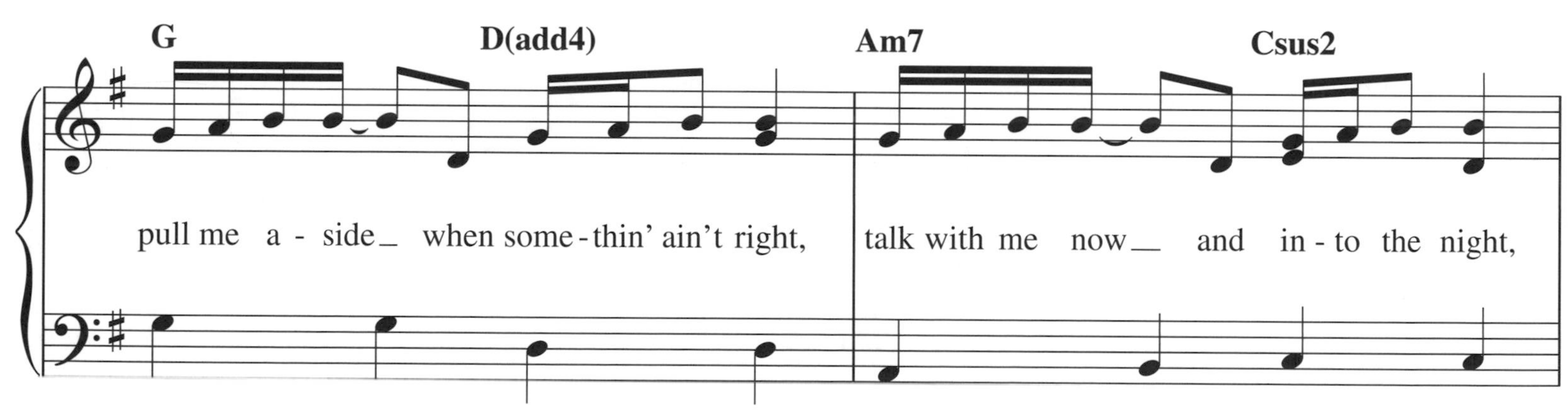
G
D(add4)
Am7
Csus2
pull me a - side when some - thin' ain't right,
talk with me now and in - to the night,

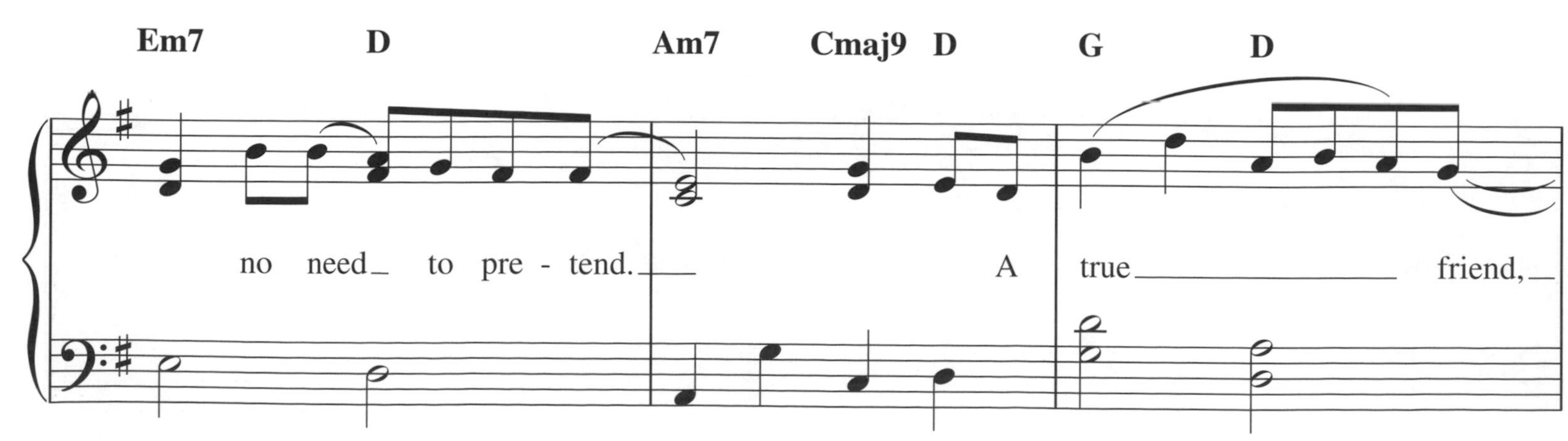
Em7
D
Am7
Cmaj9
D
G
D
no need to pre - tend. A true friend,

Am7
Csus2
G
D
C(add2)
D(add4)
you're here 'til the end. You

G
D(add4)
Am7
C
pull me a - side when some - thin' ain't right,
talk with me now and in - to the night,

Em7
D
Csus2
Gsus2
'til it's al - right a - gain.
You're a true
friend.

G
You're a true
friend.
You're a true
friend.

SEE YOU AGAIN

Words and Music by DESTINY HOPE CYRUS,
TIM JAMES and ANTONINA ARMATO

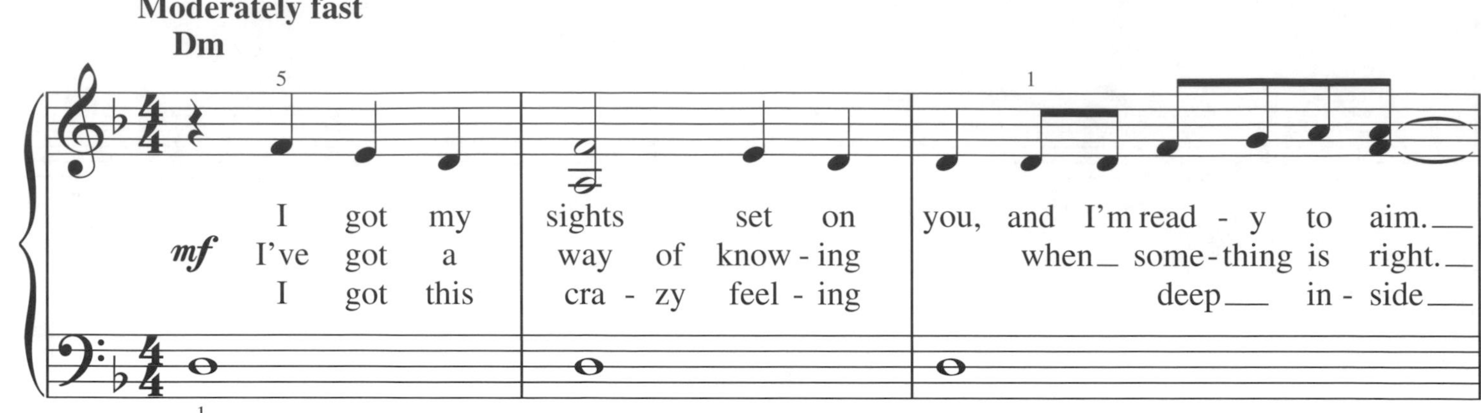

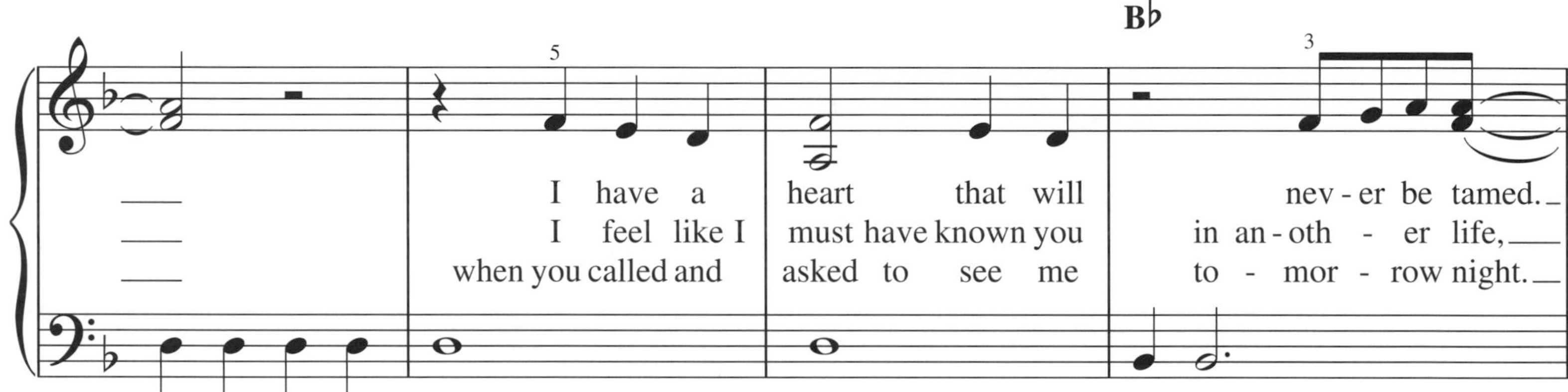

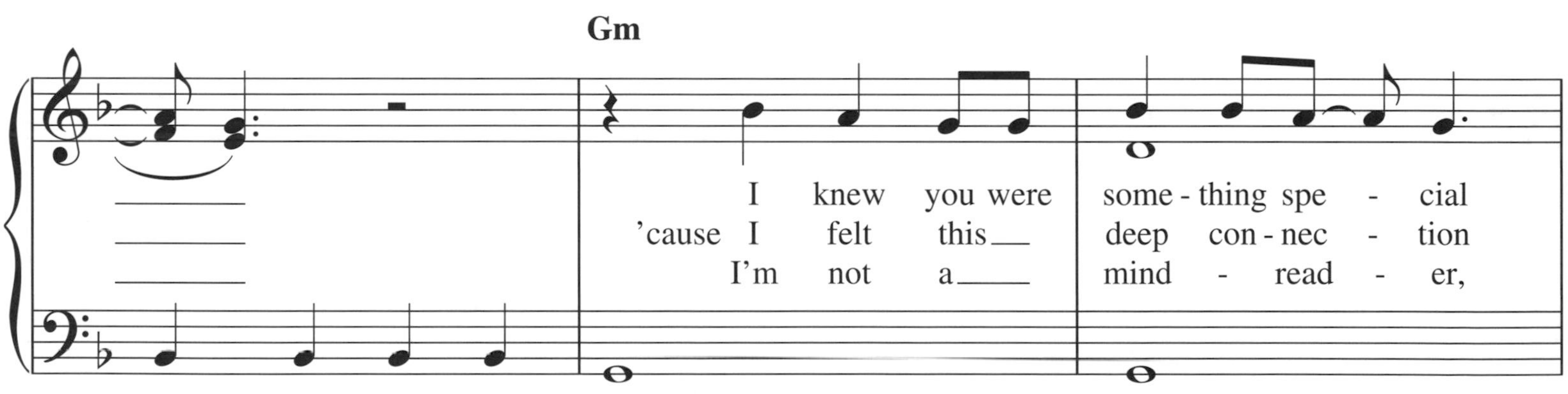

1.
2., 3.
A
Dm
to see you a - gain.
to see you a - gain.
to see me a - gain.

B♭
F
C
The last time, I freaked out;
I just kept look - ing down.
I st - st - stut - tered when you

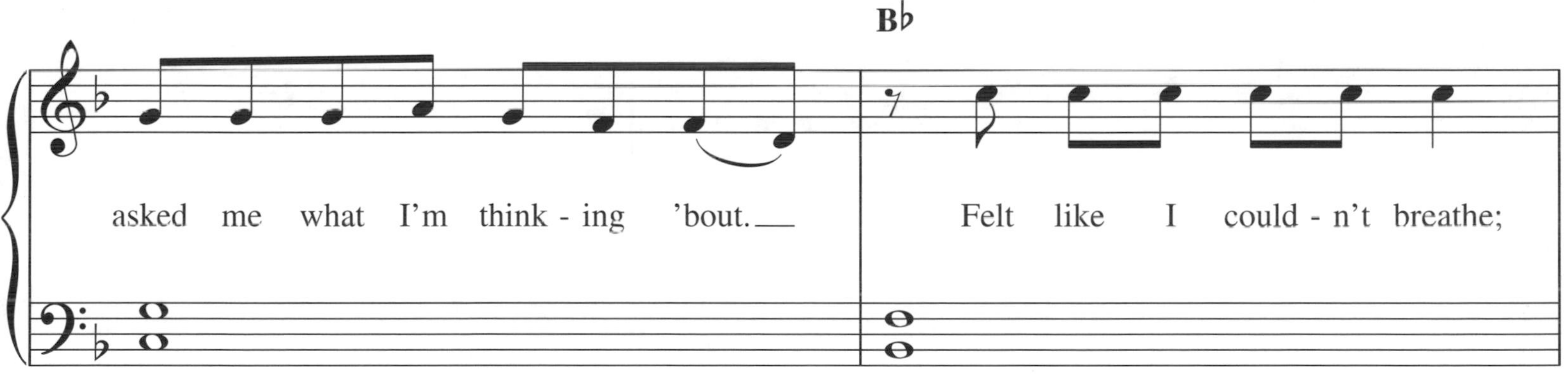
B♭
asked me what I'm think - ing 'bout.
Felt like I could - n't breathe;

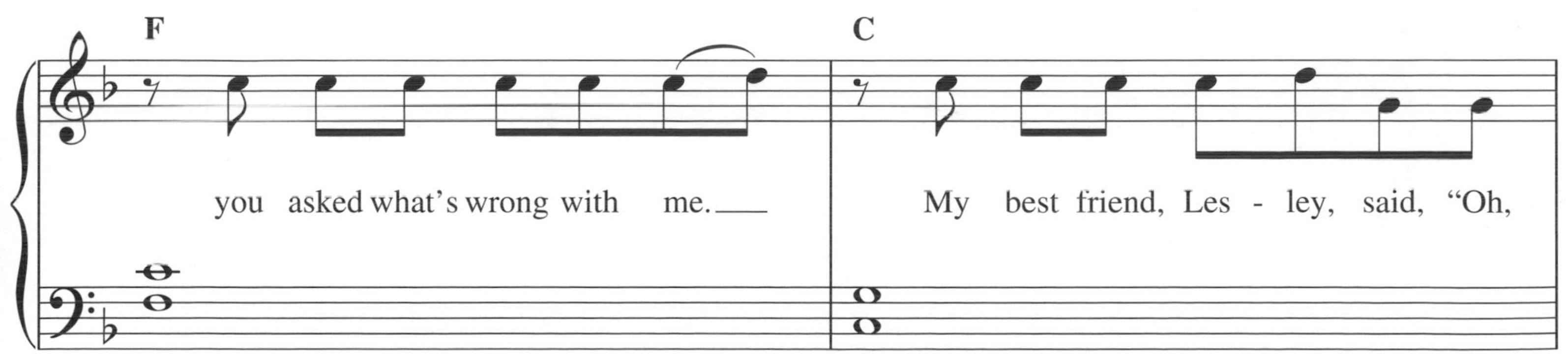
F
C
you asked what's wrong with me.
My best friend, Les - ley, said, "Oh,

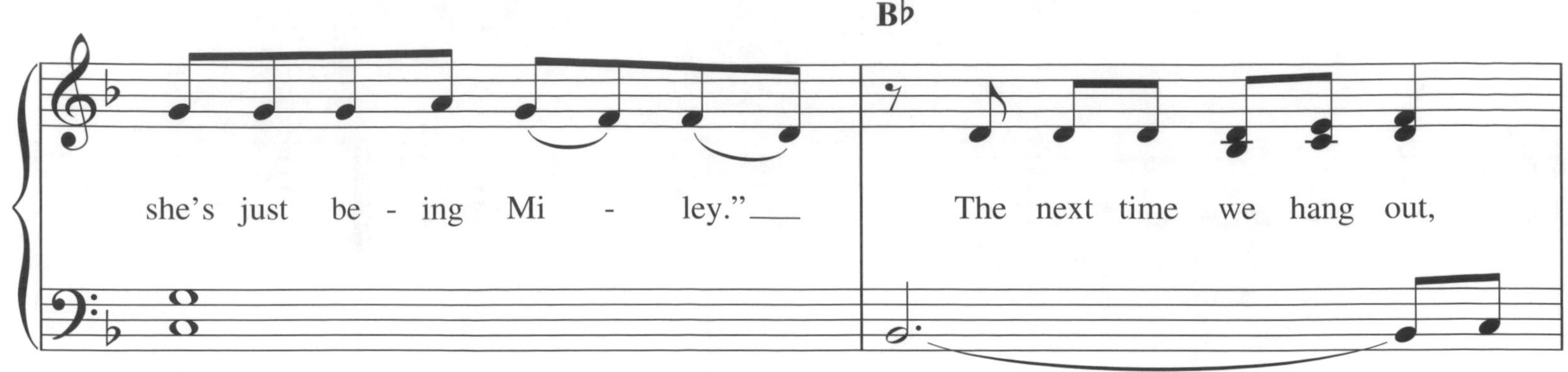
B♭
she's just be - ing Mi - ley."
The next time we hang out,

Dm
F
B♭
I will re-deem my - self.
My heart, it can't rest 'til
then. Oh, whoa, whoa,

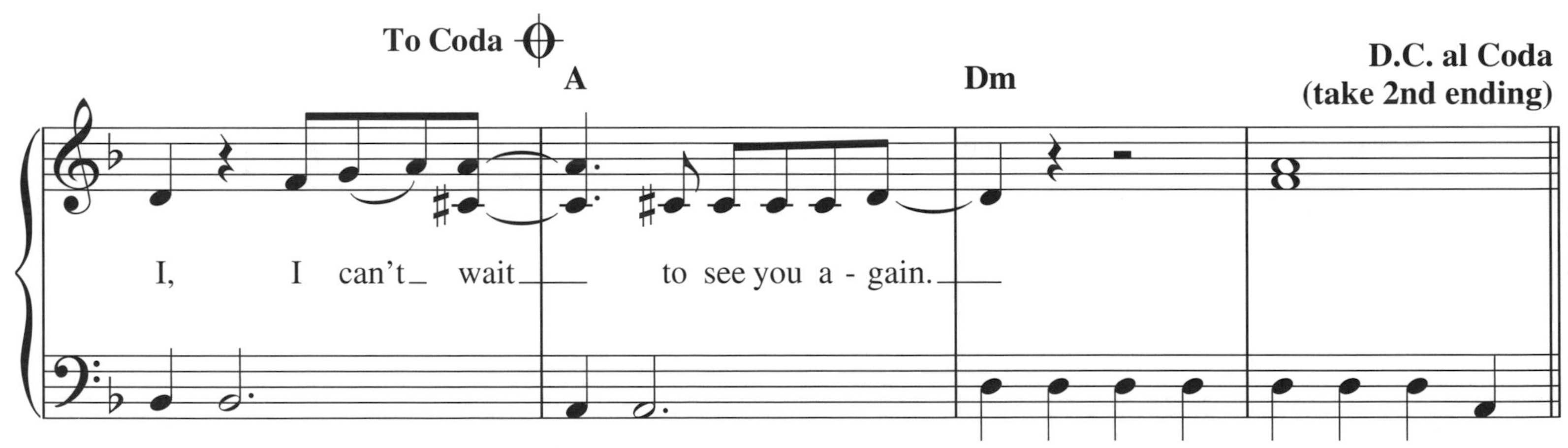
To Coda
A
Dm
D.C. al Coda
(take 2nd ending)
I, I can't wait
to see you a - gain.

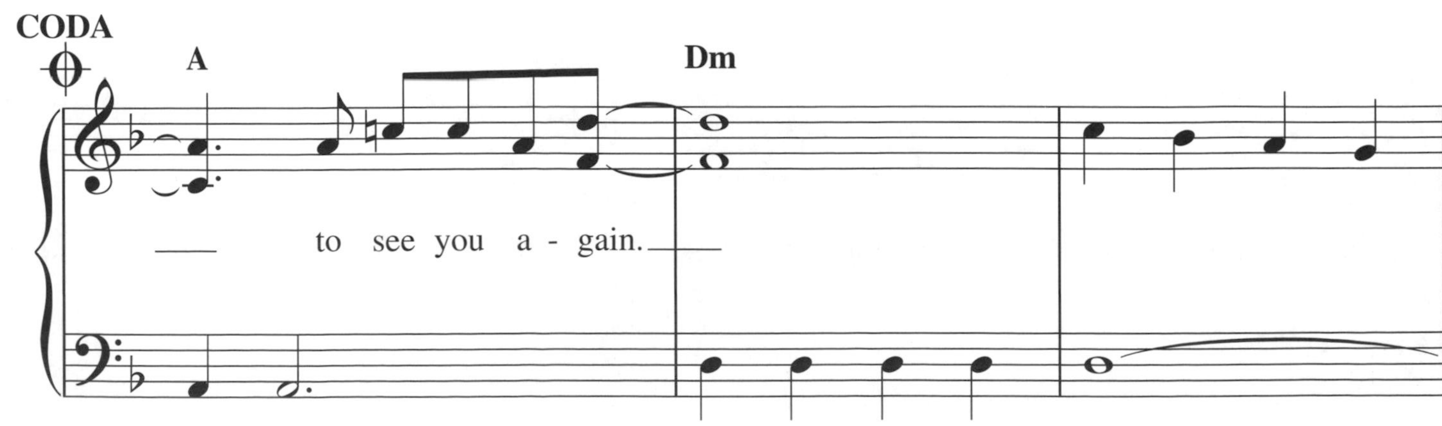
CODA
A
Dm
to see you a - gain.

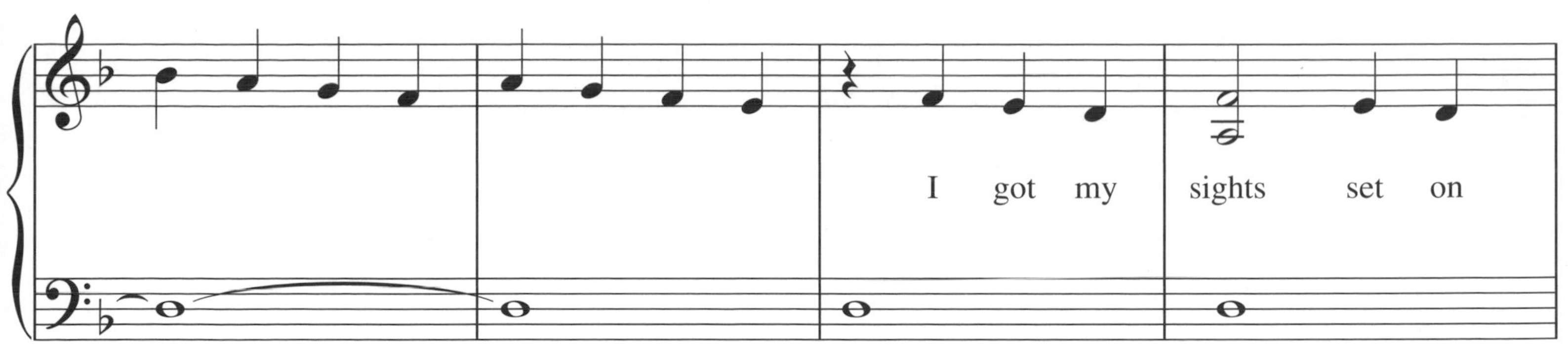
I got my sights set on

B♭
you, and I'm read - y to aim.
The last time, I freaked out;

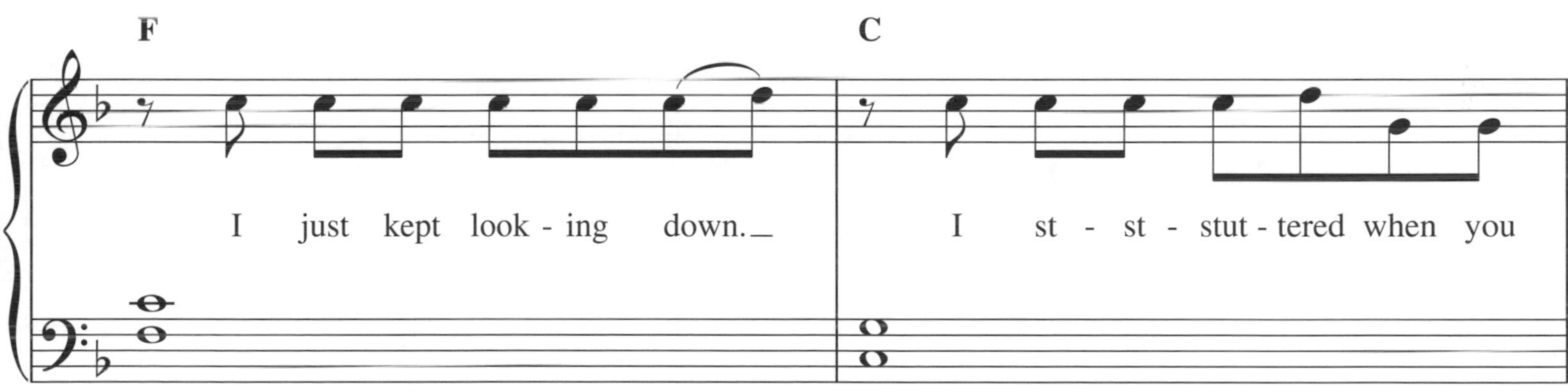
F
C
I just kept look - ing down.
I st - st - stut - tered when you

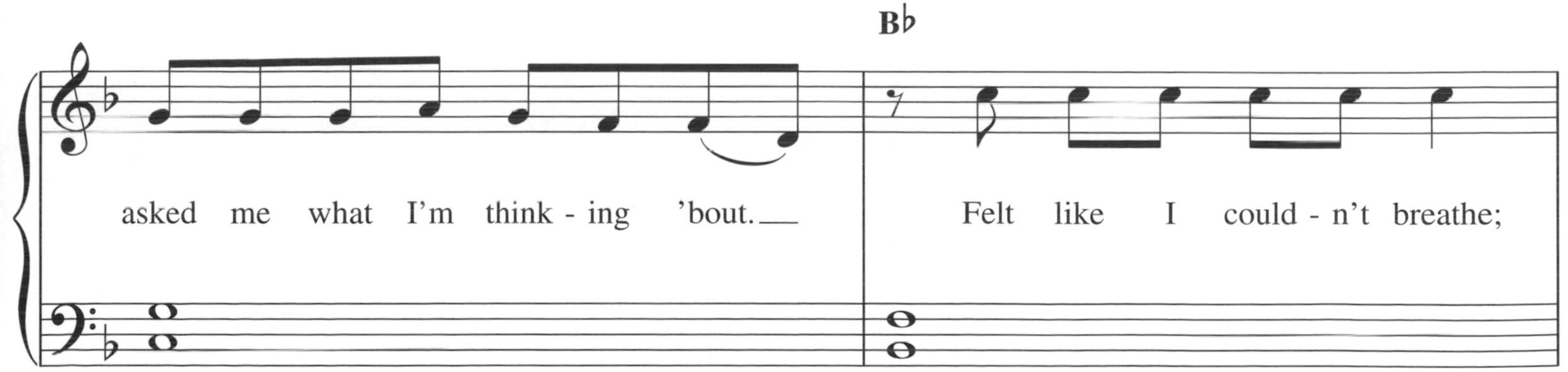
B♭
asked me what I'm think - ing 'bout.
Felt like I could - n't breathe;

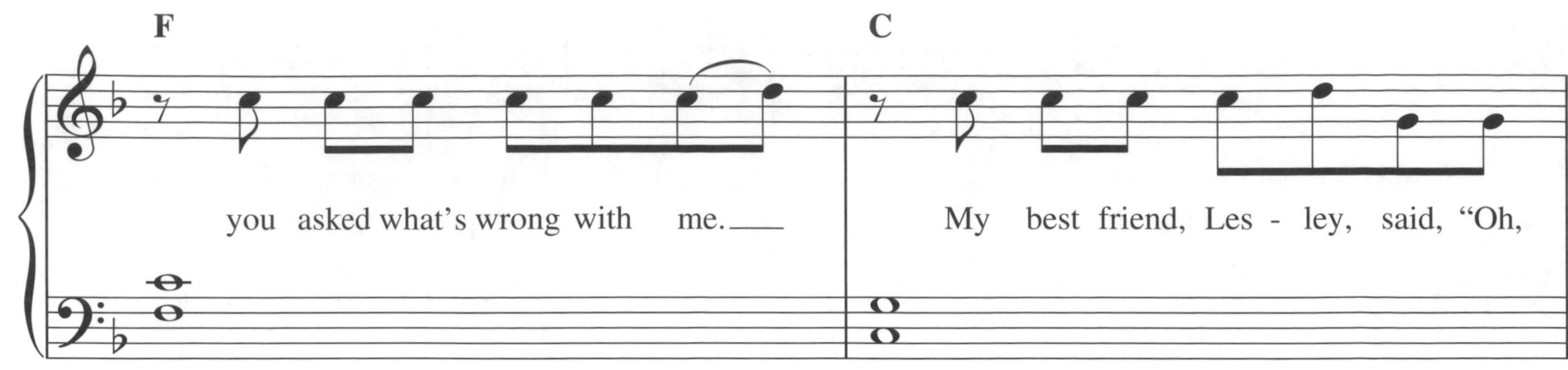
F
C
you asked what's wrong with me.
My best friend, Les - ley, said, "Oh,

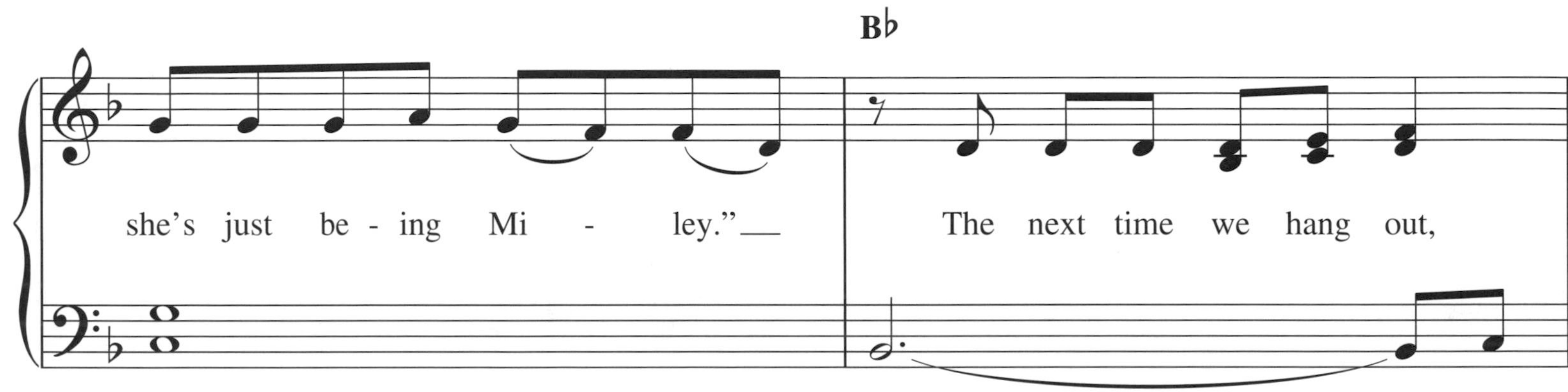
B♭
she's just be - ing Mi - ley."
The next time we hang out,

Dm
F
I will re - deem my - self.
My heart, it can't rest 'til

B♭
then. Oh, whoa, whoa,
I, I can't wait

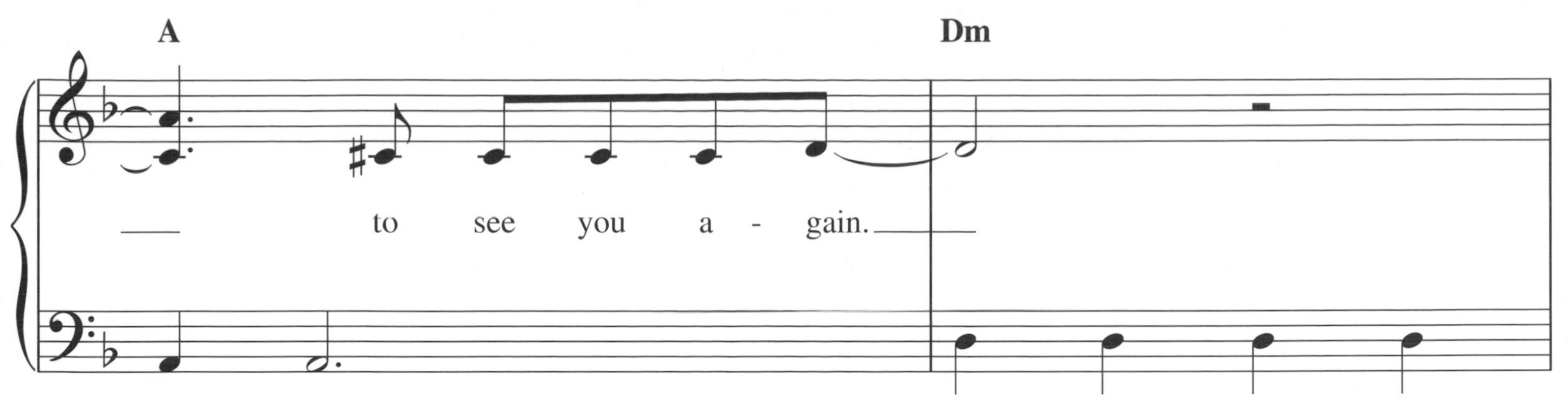
A
Dm
to see you a - gain.

B♭
Ooh, whoa, whoa, I, I can't wait

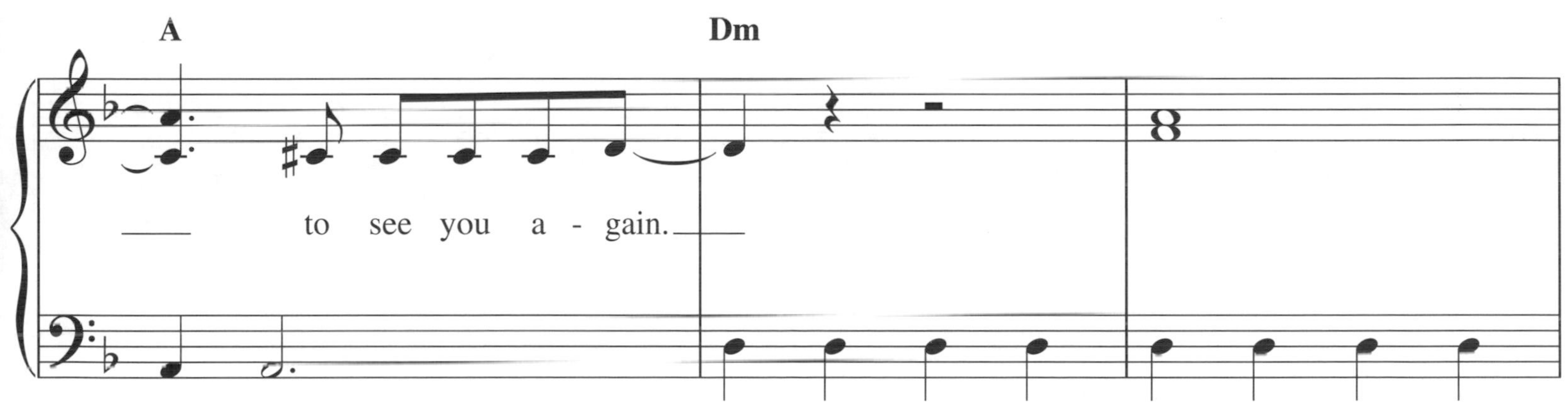
A
Dm
to see you a - gain.

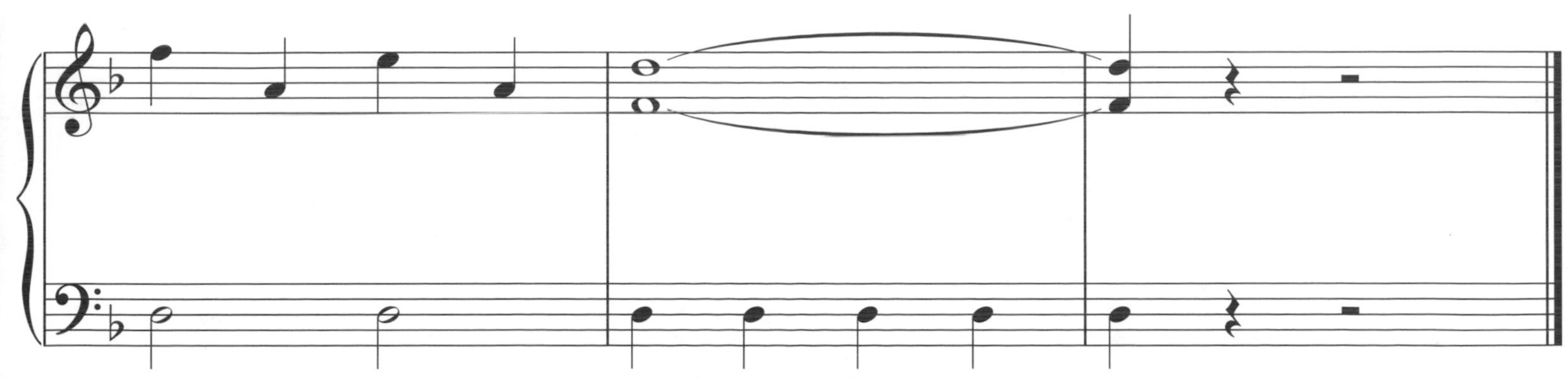

EAST NORTHUMBERLAND HIGH

Words and Music by SAMANTHA JO MOORE,
TIM JAMES and ANTONINA ARMATO

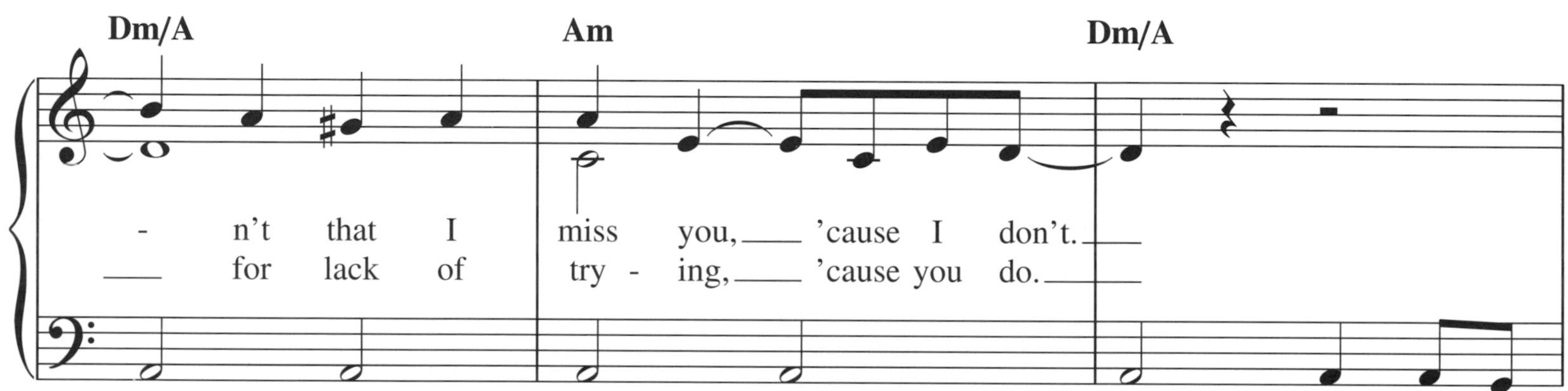

E7
Am
noth - ing that I thought you're a - bout.
things you think I want - ed to hear,
You're just caught
but you got

F
C
in a place that soon time will e - rase in my
it all wrong; I've al - read - y moved on, my

E7
F
heart.
dear.
You're my type of guy,

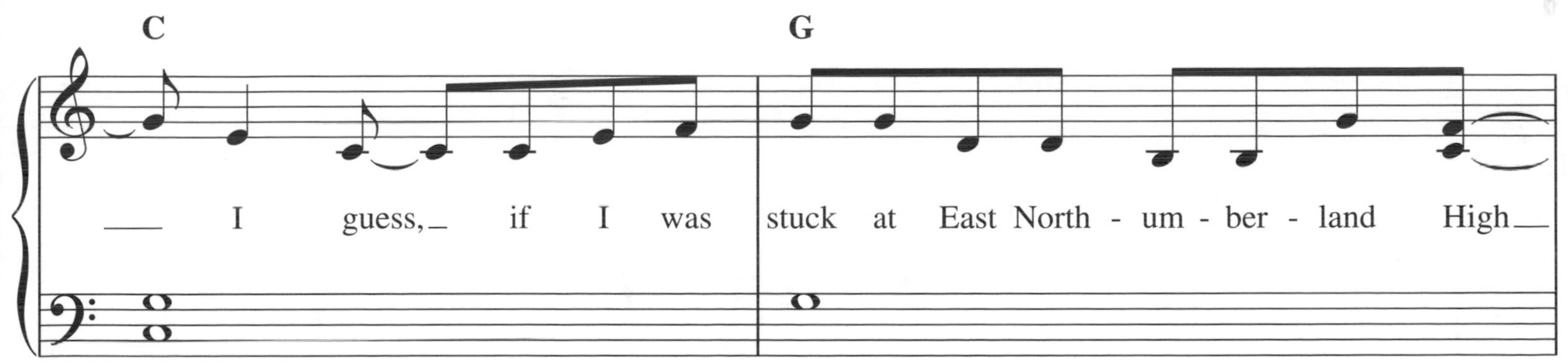
C
G
I guess, if I was stuck at East North - um - ber - land High

Dm7
F
C
for the rest of my life.
But peo-ple change:
thank God I did.

G
C
Just be-cause I liked you back then,

G
F
C
G
F
it
does-n't mean I like you now.

C
G
F
C
Just be cause I liked you back then,
it
does - n't mean I like you.

G
F
1.
Am

Dm/A
2.
C
C/B
Am7

F
Em
Dm
When you're stand - ing
near
me,

Em
I don't see so
clear - ly;
the
feel - ings are still

Dm
F
pal - pa - ble.
But when I
take two steps a - way,

C
it
sheds some light on my day.
Yeah, you

G
can't go back; it's all
in the past.
Guess
you got - ta laugh at it.

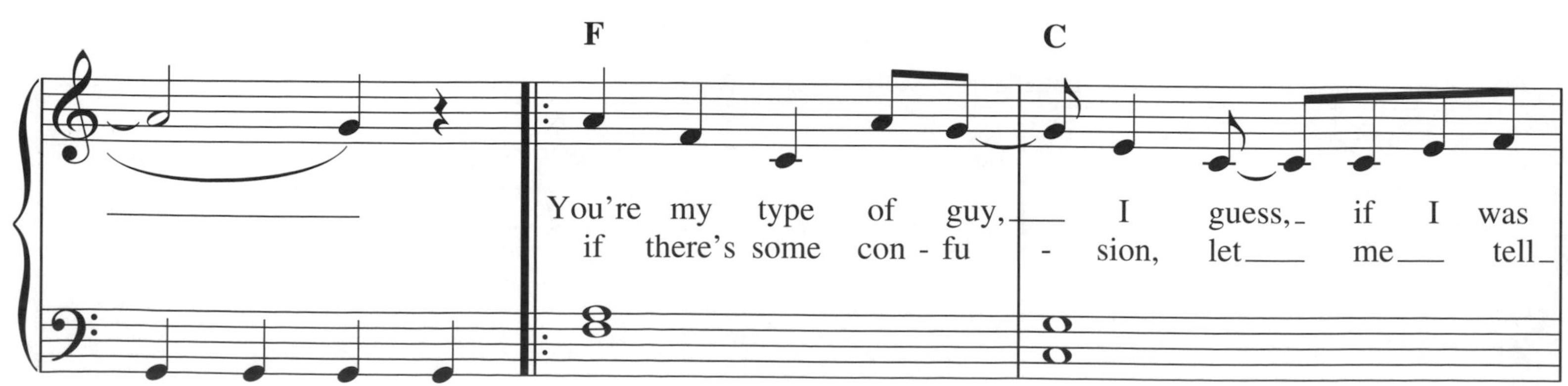
F
C
You're my type of guy,
I guess, if I was
if there's some con - fu
- sion, let me tell

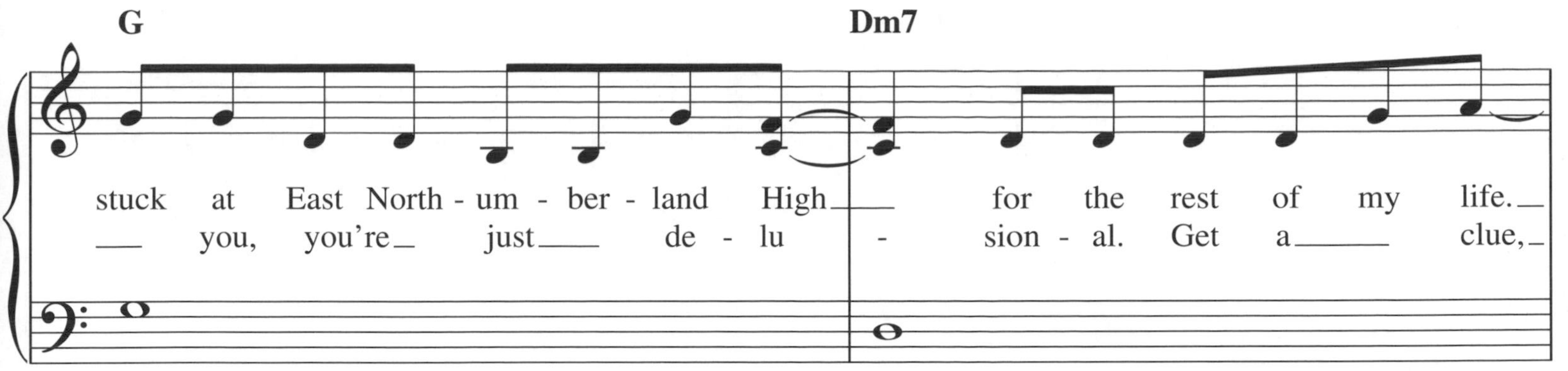
G
Dm7
stuck at East North - um - ber - land High for the rest of my life.
you, you're just de - lu - sion - al. Get a clue,

F
C
G
But 'cause peo - ple change: thank God I did.

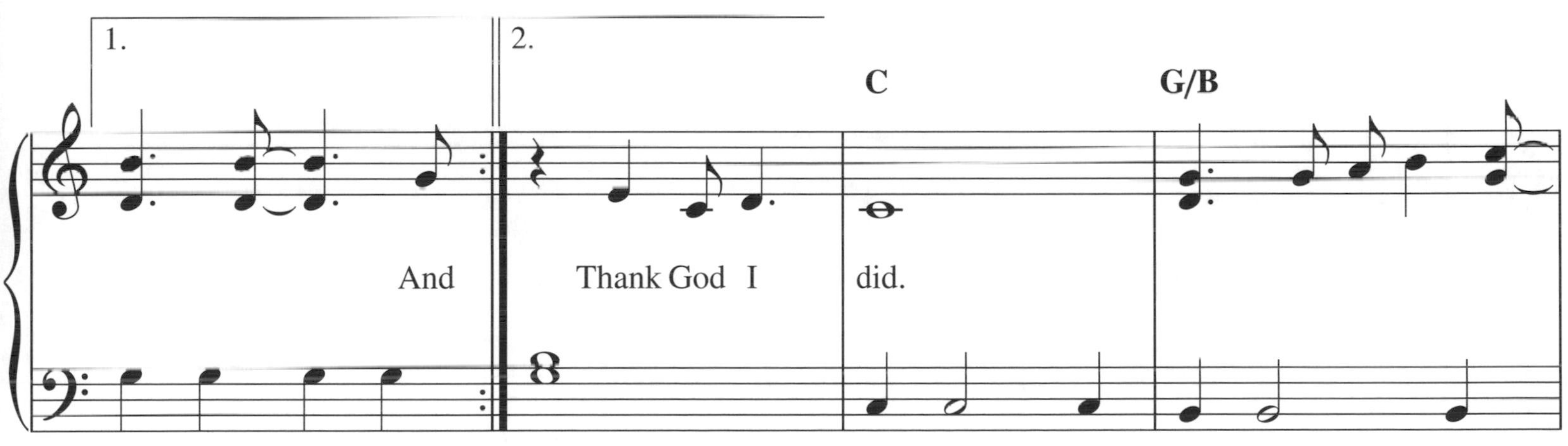
1.
2.
C
G/B
And
Thank God I did.

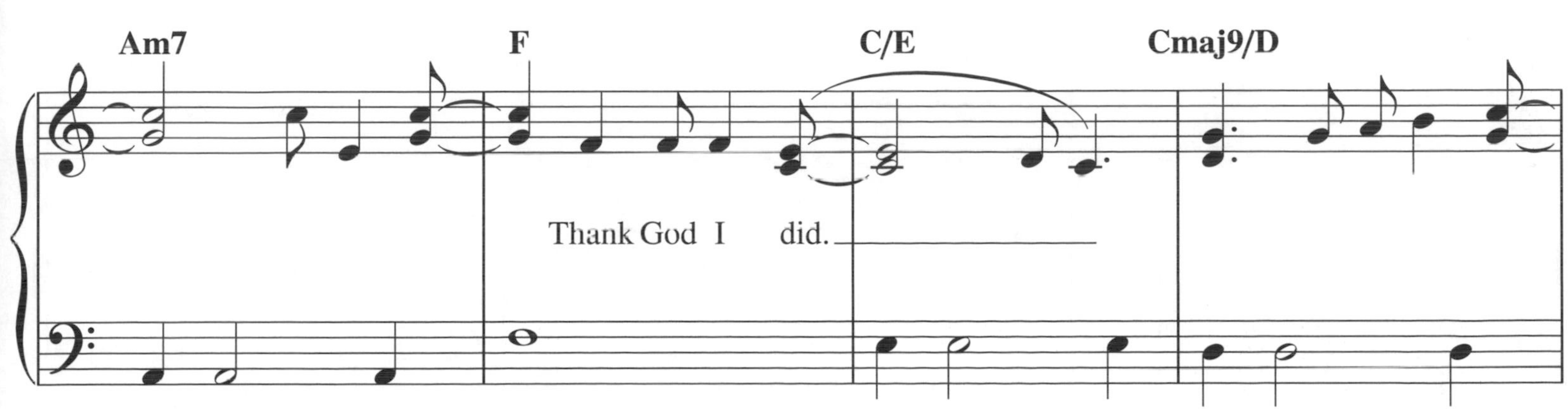
Am7
F
C/E
Cmaj9/D
Thank God I did.

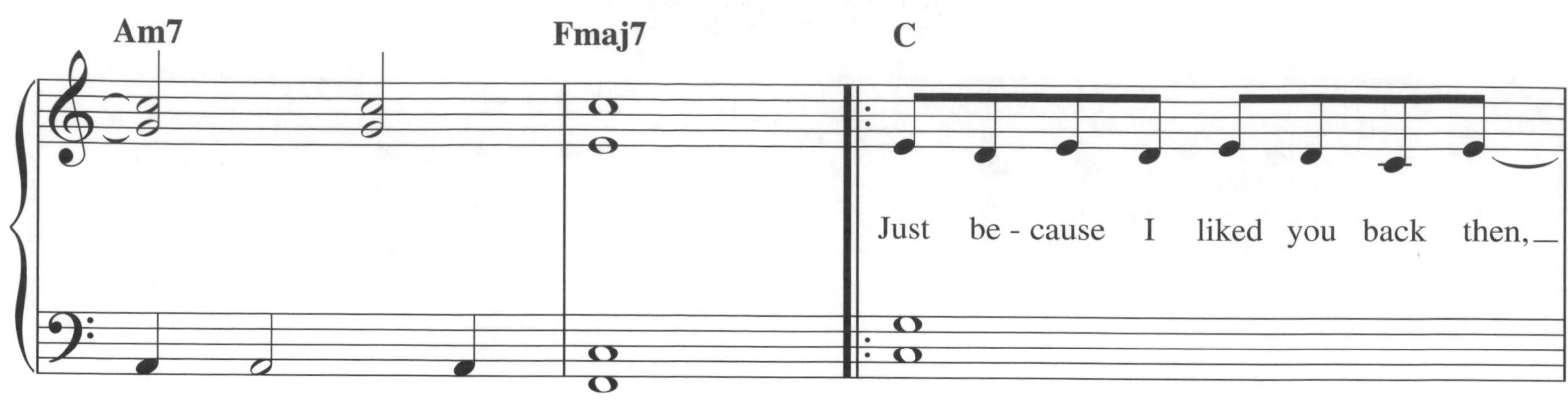
Am7
Fmaj7
C
Just be - cause I liked you back then,

G/B
1.
Am7
F
it
does-n't mean I like you now.

2.
Am7
F
C
does - n't mean I like you,
does - n't mean I like you.
Just be - cause I liked you back then,

G/B
Am7
F
it
does-n't mean I like you
now.

AS I AM

Words and Music by DESTINY HOPE CYRUS,
ALEXANDER BARRY and SHELLY PEIKEN

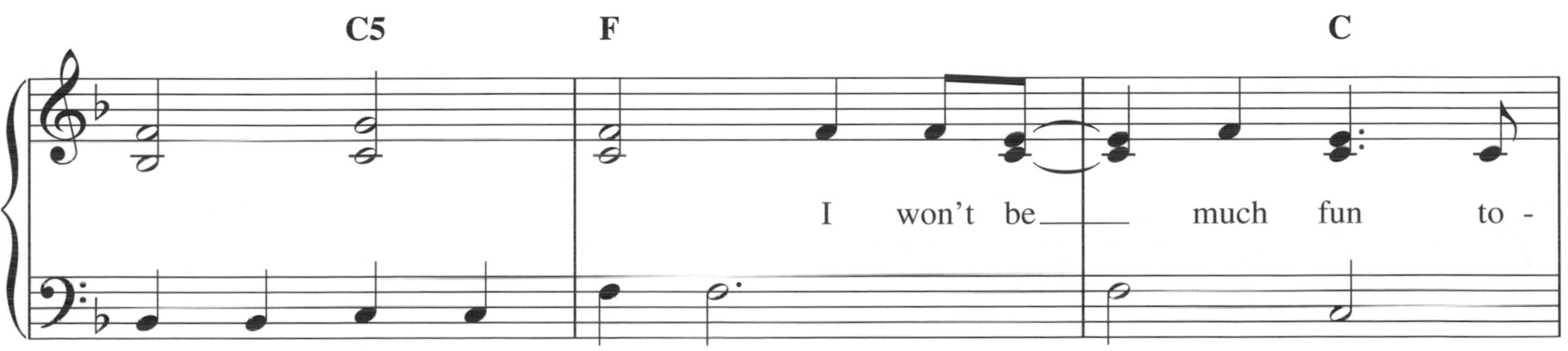

B♭
C
F
night,
and I can't be - lieve
you still

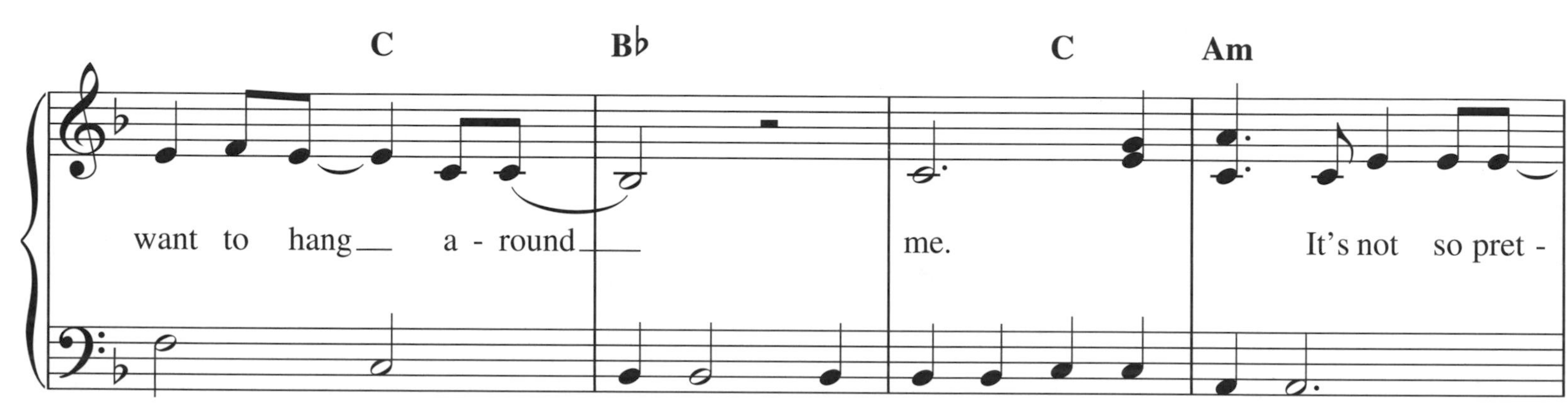
C
B♭
C
Am
want to hang a - round
me.
It's not so pret -

Dm
Am
- ty all the
time.
You don't
mind;

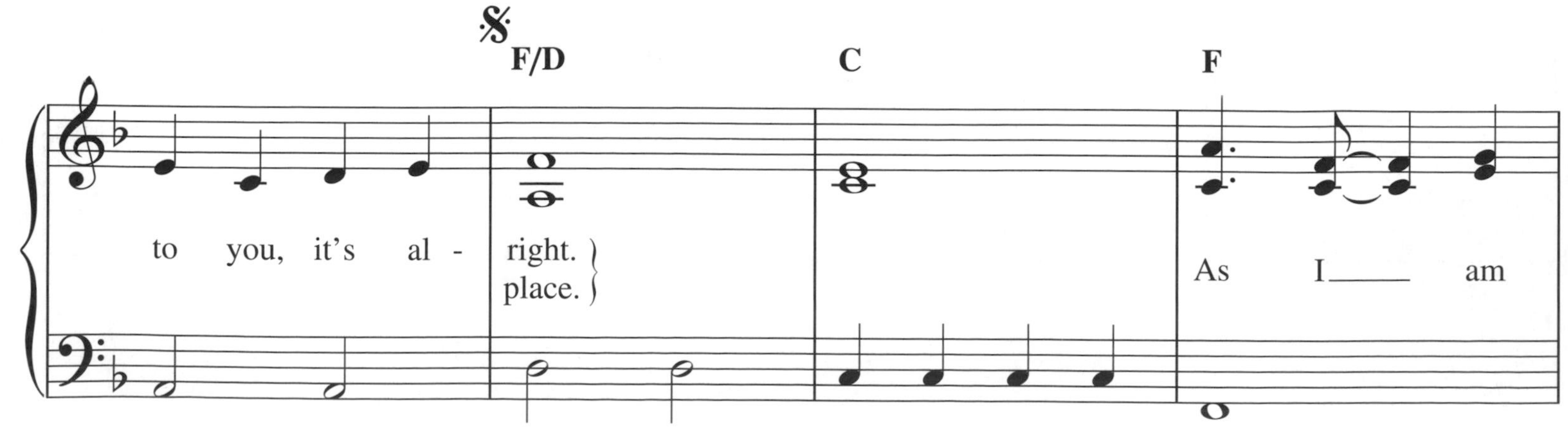
F/D
C
F
to you, it's al -
right.
place.
As I am

C
B♭
C5
F
is how you take me, nev - er try to push or make me

C
B♭
C
F5
dif - f'rent. When I talk, you lis - ten to me. As I am

C
B♭
C
F
is how you want me and I know I've found the piece that's

To Coda
C
B♭
C
F
miss - ing. I'm look - ing at him.

C
B♭
I'm not the girl you think you see, but

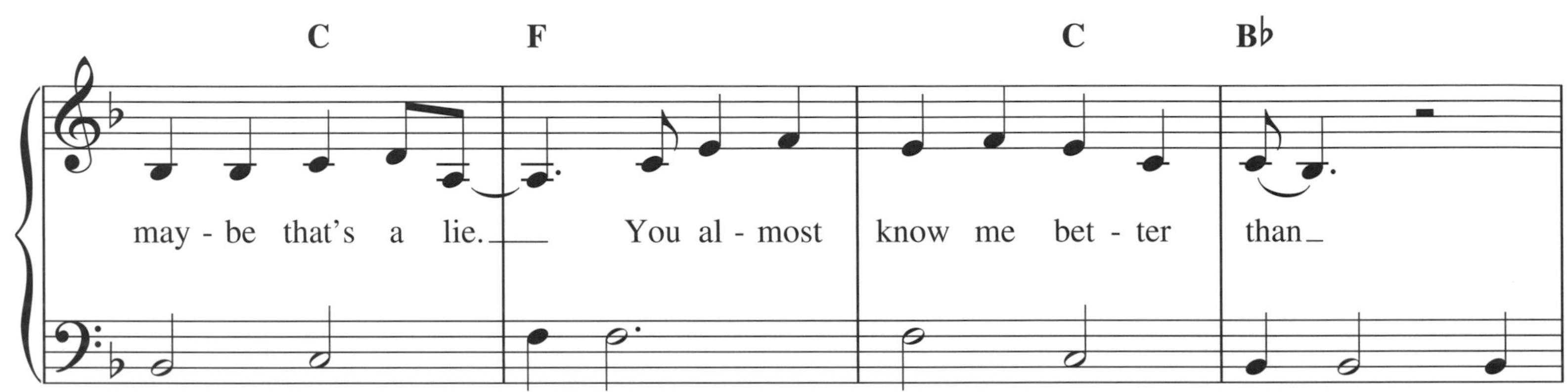
C
F
C
B♭
may - be that's a lie. You al - most know me bet - ter than

C
F
C
B♭
me, my - self and I. Don't know a lot of things, but

C
Am
Dm
I know what I've got. It's not so per - fect ev - 'ry day.

Am
D.S. al Coda
I don't have to try, 'cause it all falls in - to

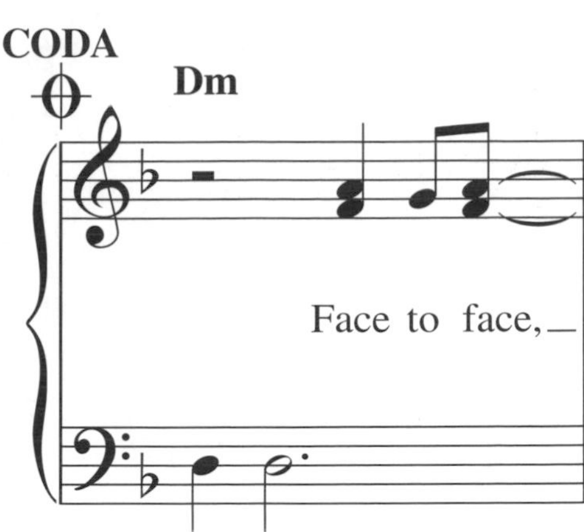
CODA
Dm
Face to face,

F
C
eye to eye, you're stand-ing there.

Fsus2/B♭
Dm
Feels good on the in - side. I don't mind,

F
C
I don't care. You're stand-ing there,

Fsus2/B♭
F
see-ing me for the first time.

F/C
F/B♭
F
See-ing me for the first time,

F/E
F/B♭
N.C.
see-ing me for the first time.
As I am

F
is how you take me, nev - er try to push or make me

C
B♭
C
F
dif - f'rent.
When I talk, you
lis - ten to me.
As I am

C
B♭
C
F
is how you
want me, and
I know I've
found the piece that's

C
B♭
C
F
miss - ing:
I'm
look - ing at him.
Found the piece that's
When I talk, you

1.
2.
C
B♭
C
C
F5
miss - ing.
lis - ten.
Take me as I
am.
am.

LET'S DANCE

Words and Music by DESTINY HOPE CYRUS,
TIM JAMES and ANTONINA ARMATO

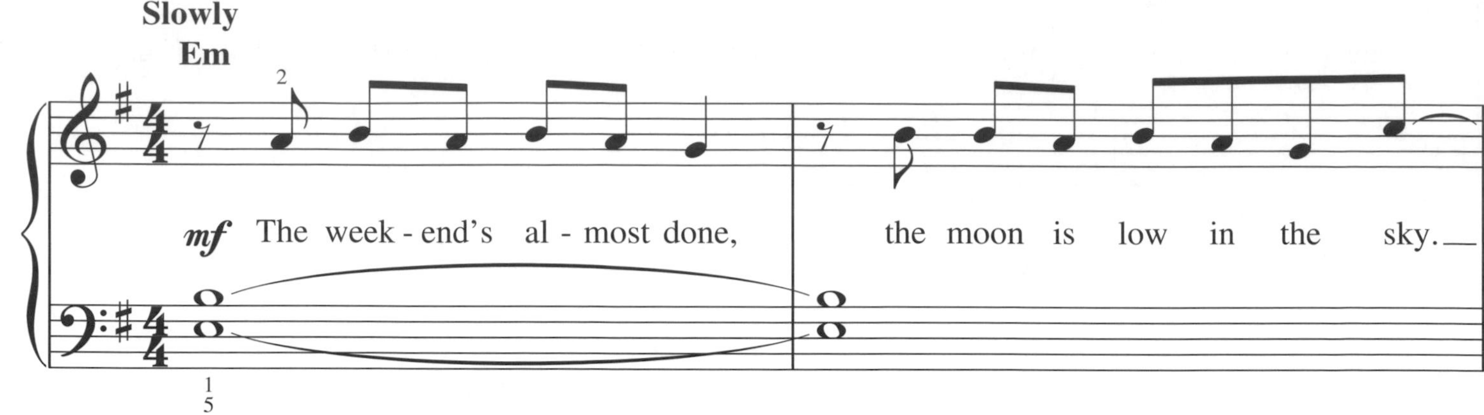

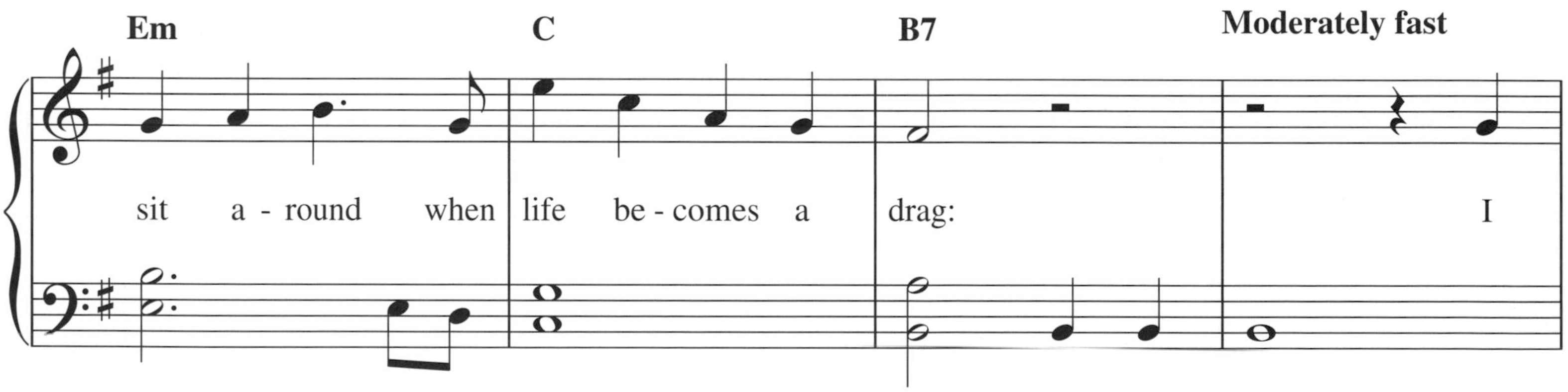

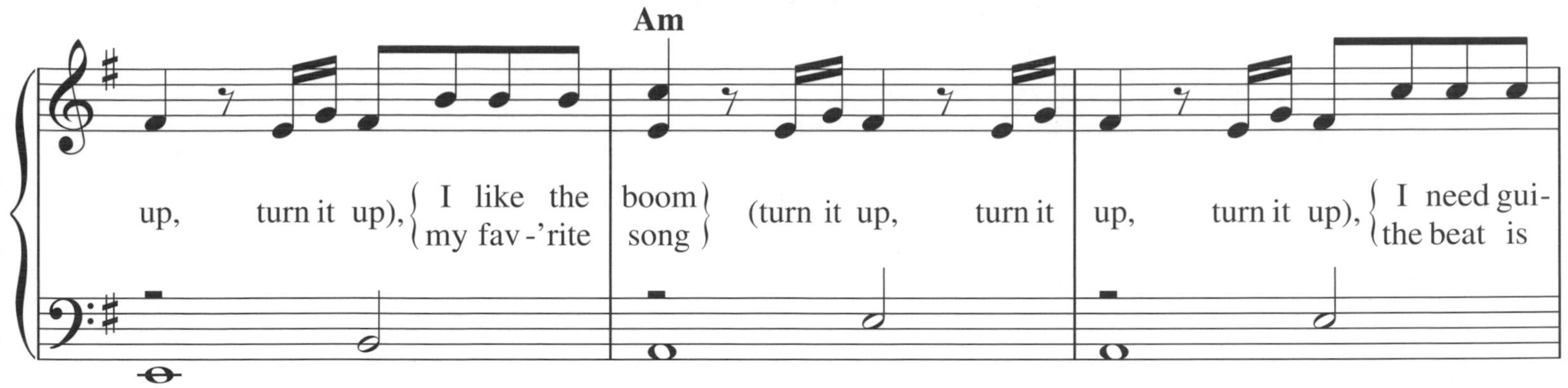
Am
up, turn it up), I like the boom (turn it up, turn it up, turn it up), I need gui-
my fav-'rite song the beat is

B7
Em N.C.
tar (turn it up, turn it up, turn it up), I like the drum when it goes,
strong (turn it up, turn it up, turn it up), we'll dance.

Em
"Bm-d'-bm - d' - bm." Let's dance, what the week-end, what the night is all a-bout. Let's

Am7
dance: grab your girl-friends, grab your boy-friends, let it out. Let's

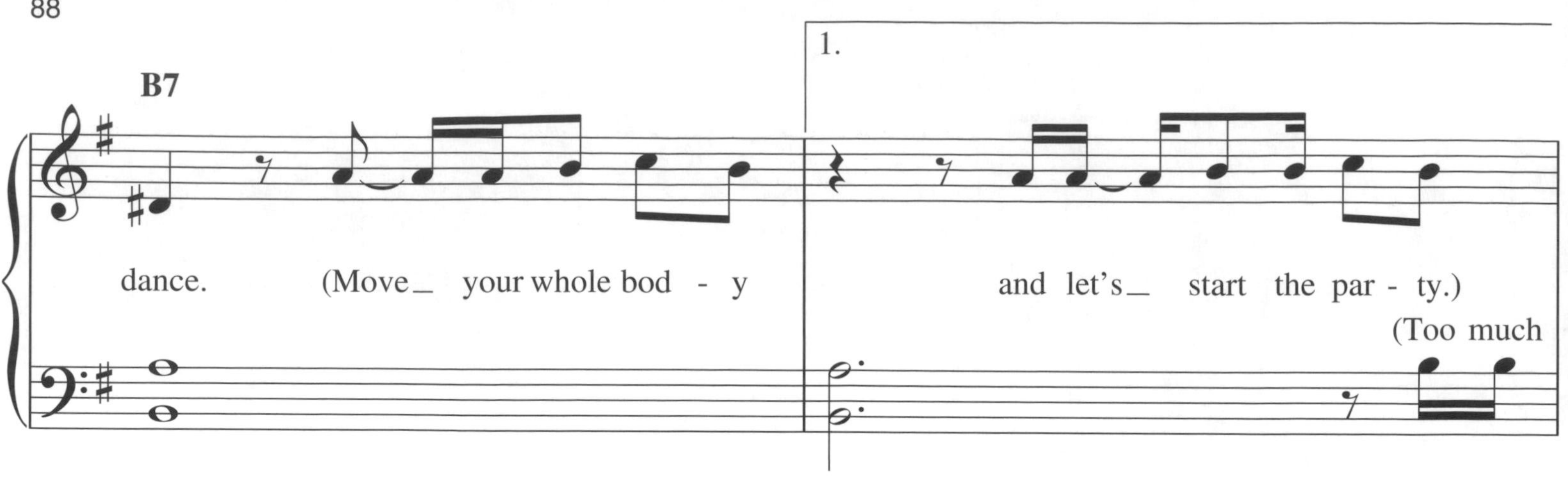
B7
1.
dance. (Move_ your whole bod - y
and let's_ start the par - ty.)
(Too much

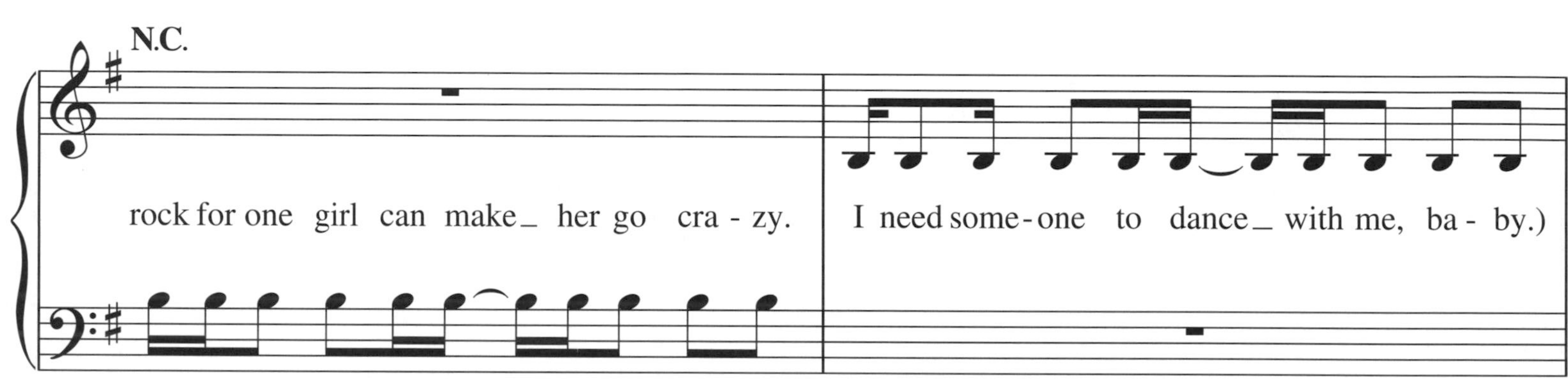
N.C.
rock for one girl can make_ her go cra - zy.
I need some-one to dance_ with me, ba - by.)

Em
2.
Dance! The mu - sic's
and let's_ start the par - ty.

N.C.
Em
I need some-one to dance_with me, ba- by.)
Dance!
When the night

Am
says hel - lo, yeah, get read - y to go. Turn it up, turn it loose, yeah, you've got

B7
no ex - cuse. Just take a chance, get out on the floor and dance.

Em
Let's dance, what the week - end, what the

Am
night is all a - bout. Let's dance: grab your girl - friends, grab your boy - friends, let it out. Let's

1.
B7
Em
dance. (And let's start the par - ty.) Dance with me, dance with me,

2.
B7
dance with me, dance. Let's
dance. Move your whole bod - y

N.C.
and let's start the par - ty. Soon as my al - bum goes num - ber one, we'll start

Em
liv - in' like a roll - er with for - ty dia - monds.

START ALL OVER

Words and Music by FEFE DOBSON,
SCOTT CUTLER and ANNE PREVIN

F
C
A7
It's soon - er than I
thought, but you called me
want, but you caught my

F
C
out.
heart.
I lost con - trol, and there's no
I guess I'm read - y now to

E♭
G
doubt
start.
I'm gon - na start all o - ver.
Out of the fire and

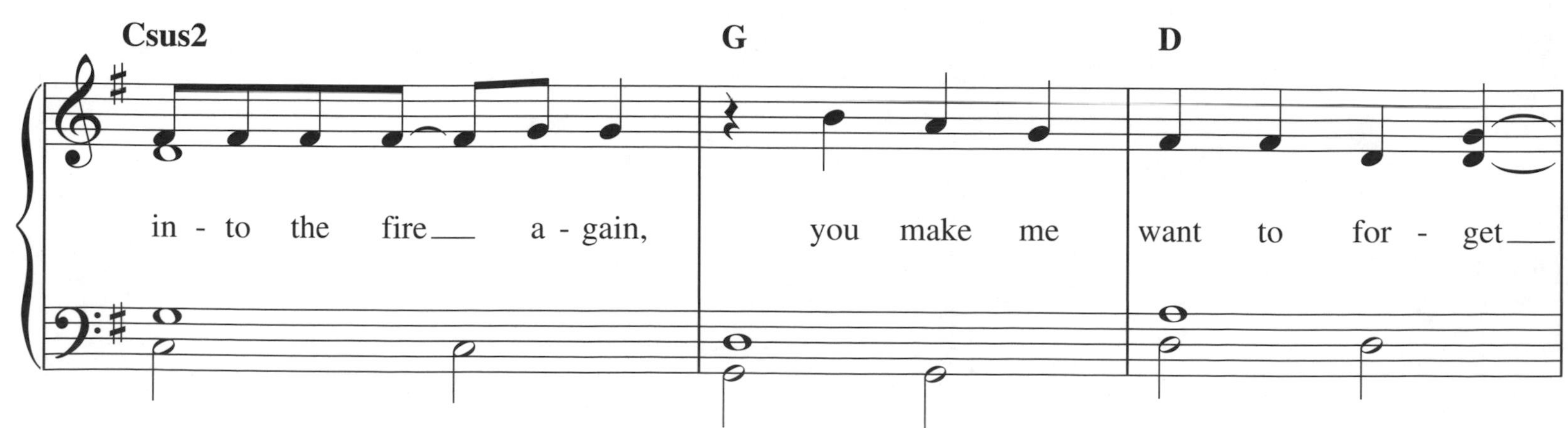
Csus2
G
D
in - to the fire a - gain, you make me want to for - get

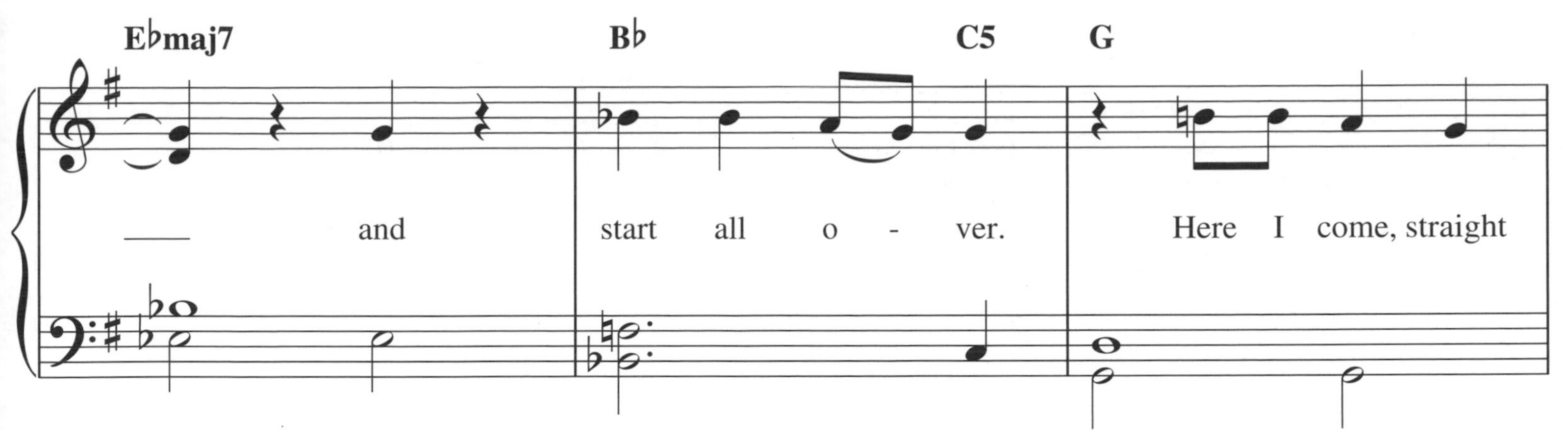

E♭maj7
B♭
C5
G
and start all o - ver.
Here I come, straight

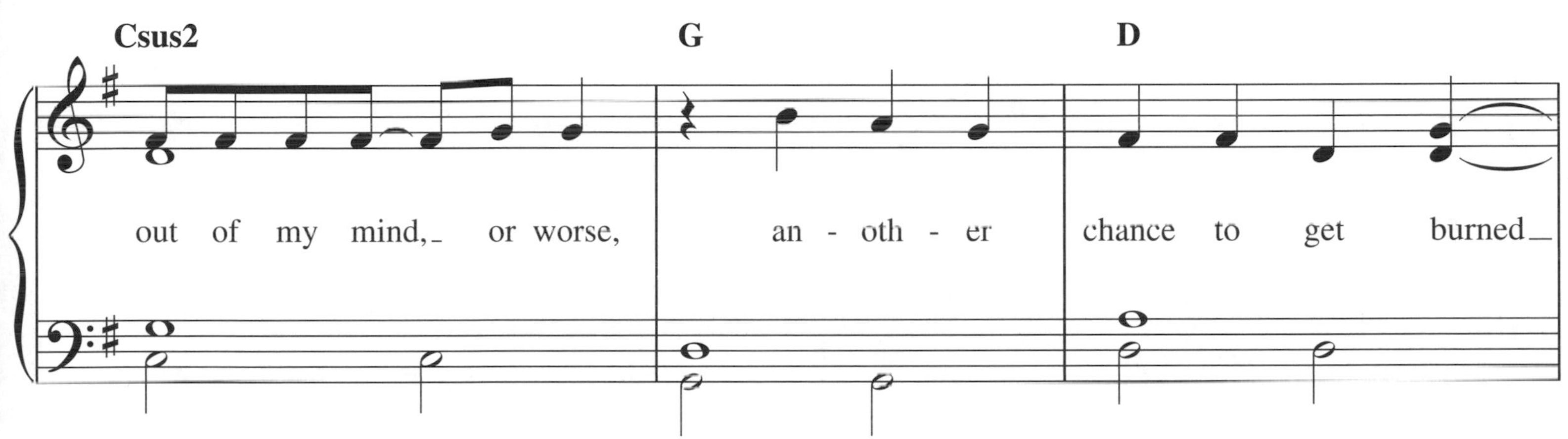

Csus2
G
D
out of my mind, or worse,
an - oth - er
chance to get burned

E♭maj7
B♭
C5
E♭
To Coda
and start all o - ver.
I'm gon - na

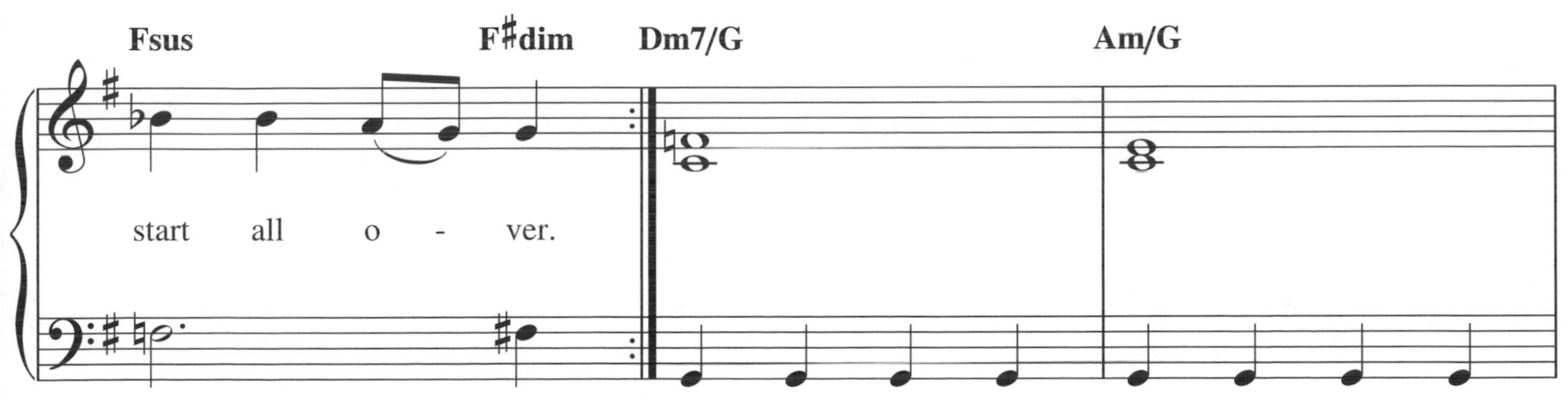

Fsus
F♯dim
Dm7/G
Am/G
start all o - ver.

G6
Dm/G
It's so eas - y, you dis -

Am/G
G6
rupt me, can't com - plain. It's so

Dm/G
Am/G
G
eas - y, you dis - rupt me, can't com - plain.

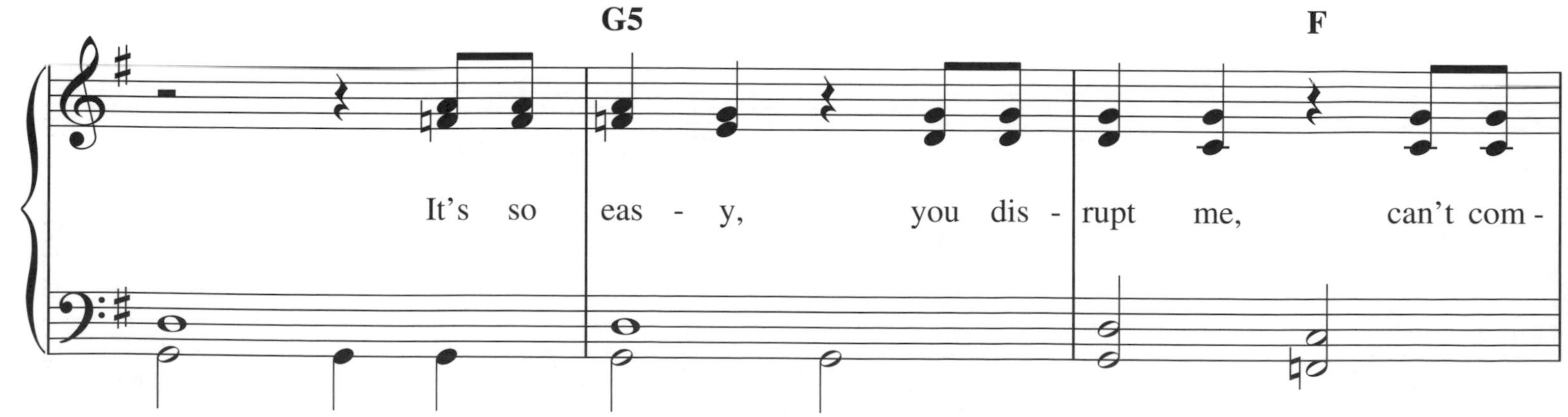
G5
F
It's so eas - y, you dis - rupt me, can't com -

G
F5
G5
plain.
It's so eas - y.
F
E♭maj7/G
I'm gon - na start all o - ver
N.C.
D.S. al Coda
(start all o - ver).
CODA
Fsus
F♯dim
G5
start all o - ver.

G.N.O.
(Girl's Night Out)

Words and Music by MATTHEW WILDER
and TAMARA DUNN

2.
Gm
Dm
Send out a 9 - 1 - 1:
we're gon - na
Gm
have some fun.
Hey, boy, you know you bet - ter run,
C
F
'cause it's a girl's night, it's al -
- right with - out you.
C
I'm gon - na stay

Dm
C
out and play out with - out you.

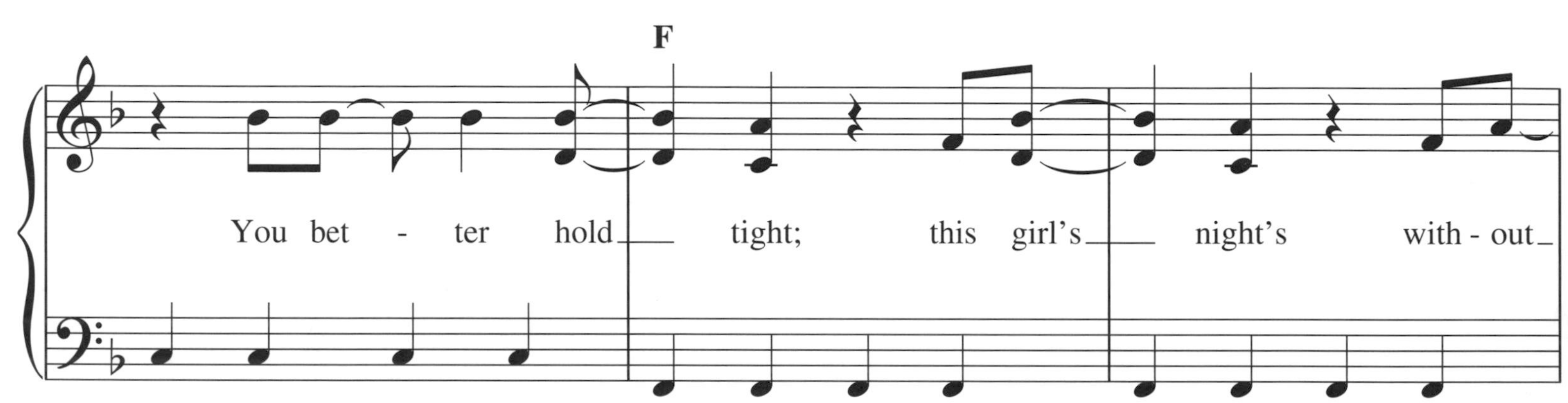
F
You bet - ter hold tight; this girl's night's with - out

C
Gm
you.
Let's go, a G. N. O.

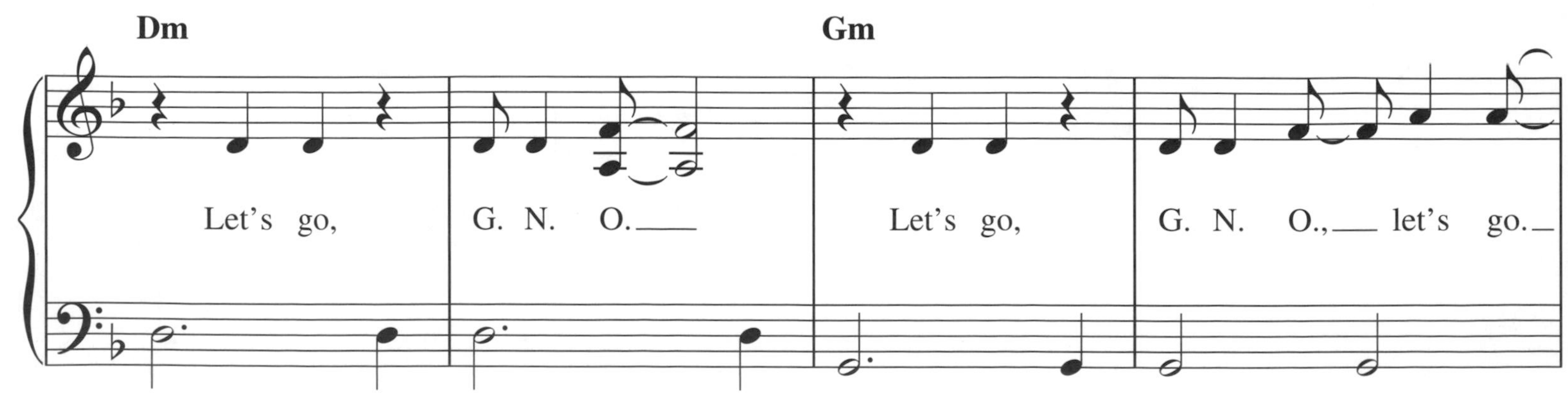
Dm
Gm
Let's go, G. N. O. Let's go, G. N. O., let's go.

To Coda
C
Dm
It's a girl's night.

Gm
Am
B♭
I'll dance with some - bod - y new,
won't have to think

C
F
a - bout you, and who knows
what "Let go" will lead

C
Gm
to.
You'll hear from ev - 'ry - one,

Dm
Gm
you'll get the 4 - 1 - 1.
Hey, boy, you

C
knew this day would come,
'cause it's a girl's

F
C
night, it's al - right with - out you.

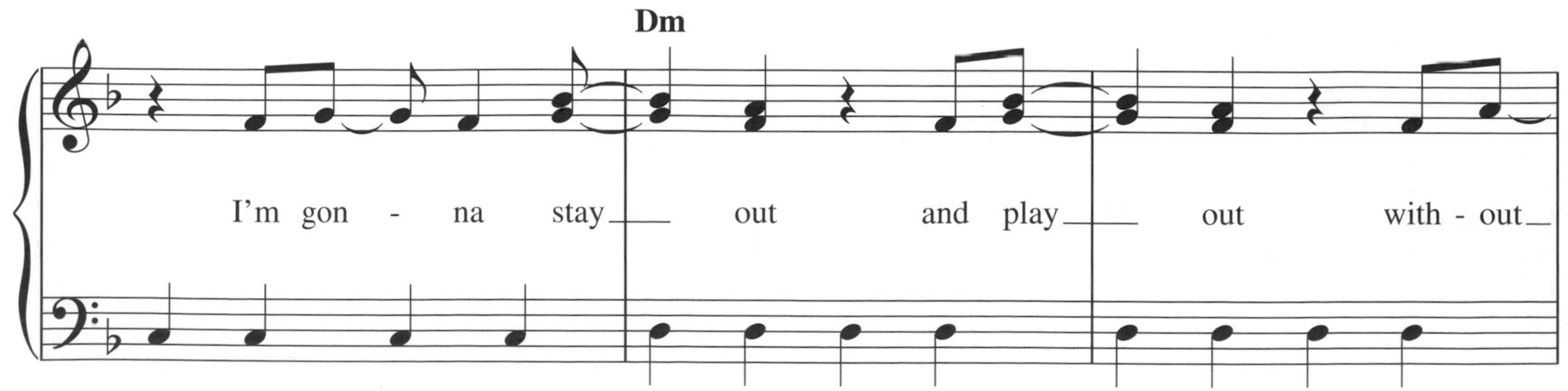
Dm
I'm gon - na stay out and play out with - out

C
Gm
you.
Let's go, a
G. N. O.

Dm
Gm
Let's go,
G. N. O.
Let's go,

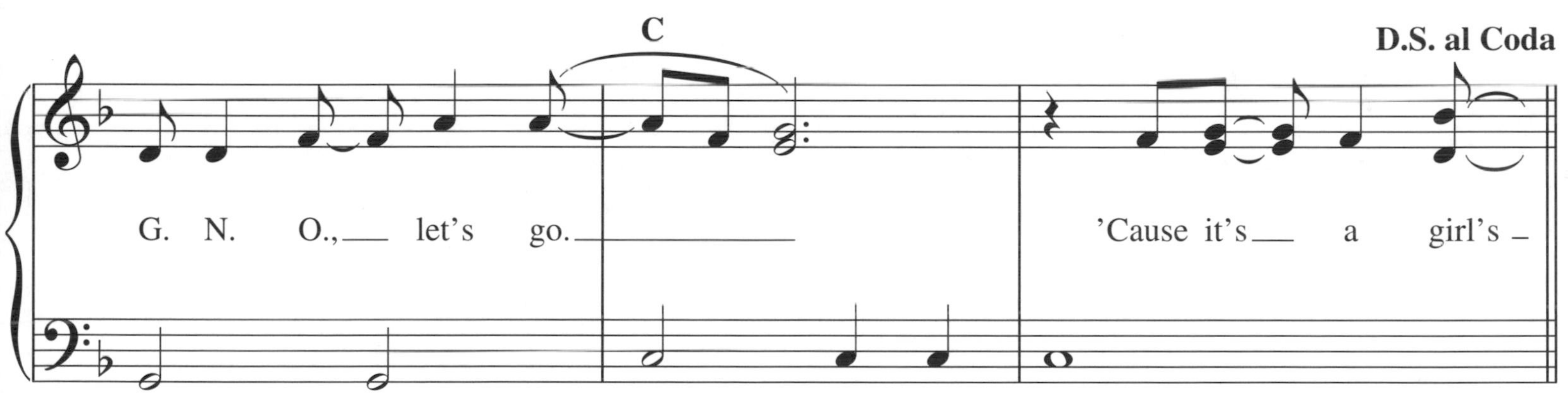
C
D.S. al Coda
G. N. O., let's go.
'Cause it's a girl's

CODA
Dm

RIGHT HERE

Words and Music by DESTINY HOPE CYRUS,
TIM JAMES and ANTONINA ARMATO

Moderately fast

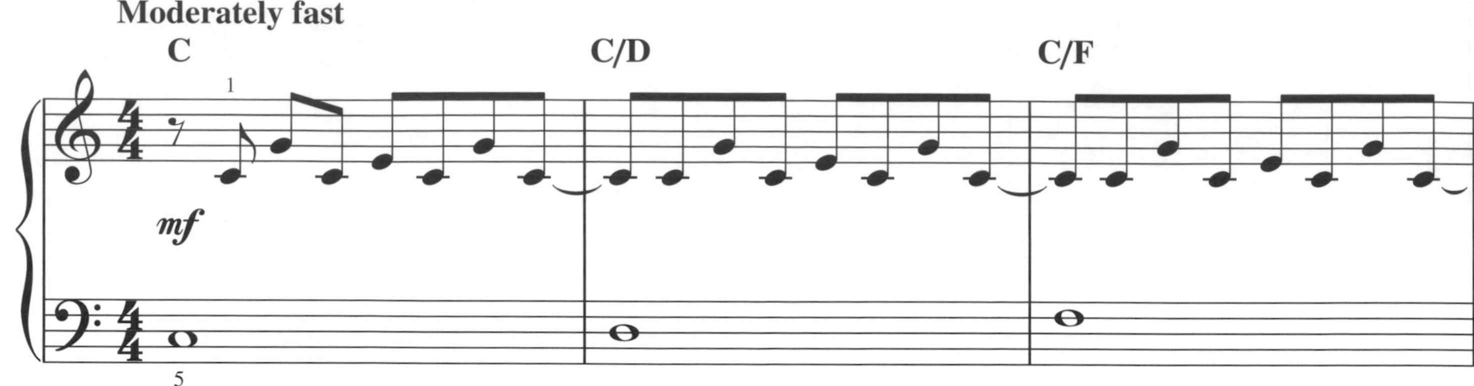

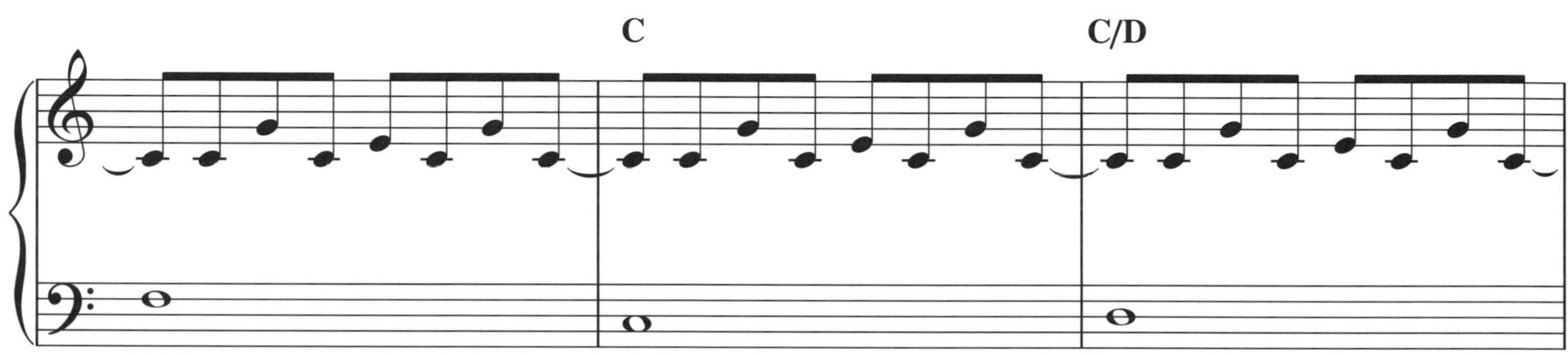

C/F
1.
C
be
right
here.
If you
2.
C
here.
All you have to
Asus2
F5
C5
do is call my name,
no mat-ter how
close or far a - way.
G5
A5
F5
Ask me once
and I'll come,
I'll come run -

C5
G
Asus2
- ning.
And when I can't be
with you, dream me near;

F5
C5
G5
keep me in your
heart and I'll ap - pear.
All you got - ta

F5
To Coda
do is turn a - round, close your
eyes, look in - side.
I'm right here.

C/F
C
Is - n't it great
that you know

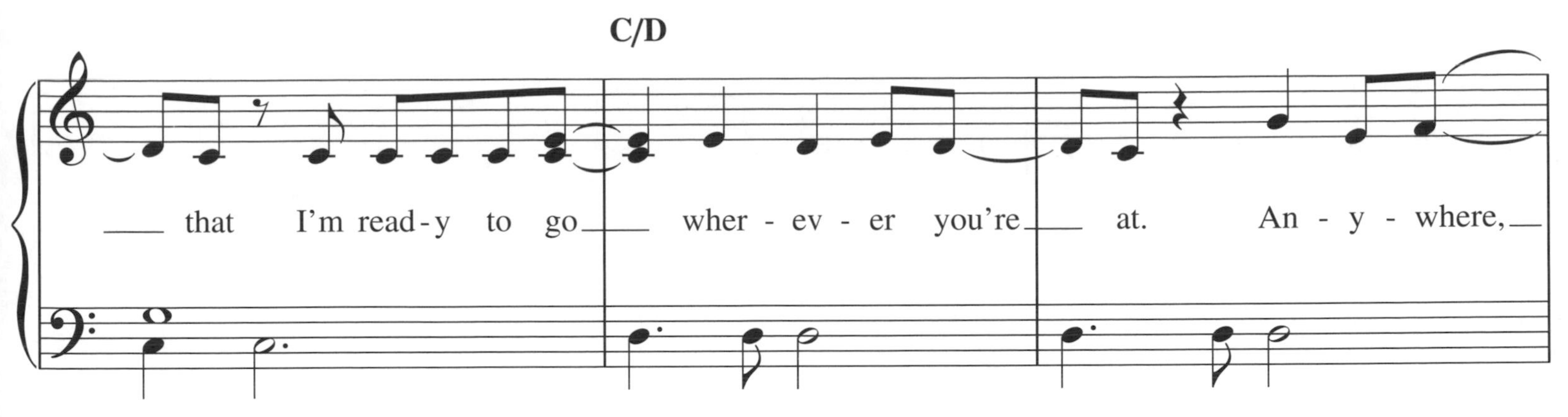
C/D
that I'm read-y to go wher - ev - er you're at. An - y - where,

C/F
C
I'll be there.

D.S. al Coda
All you have to

CODA
Cmaj7
I'm right here

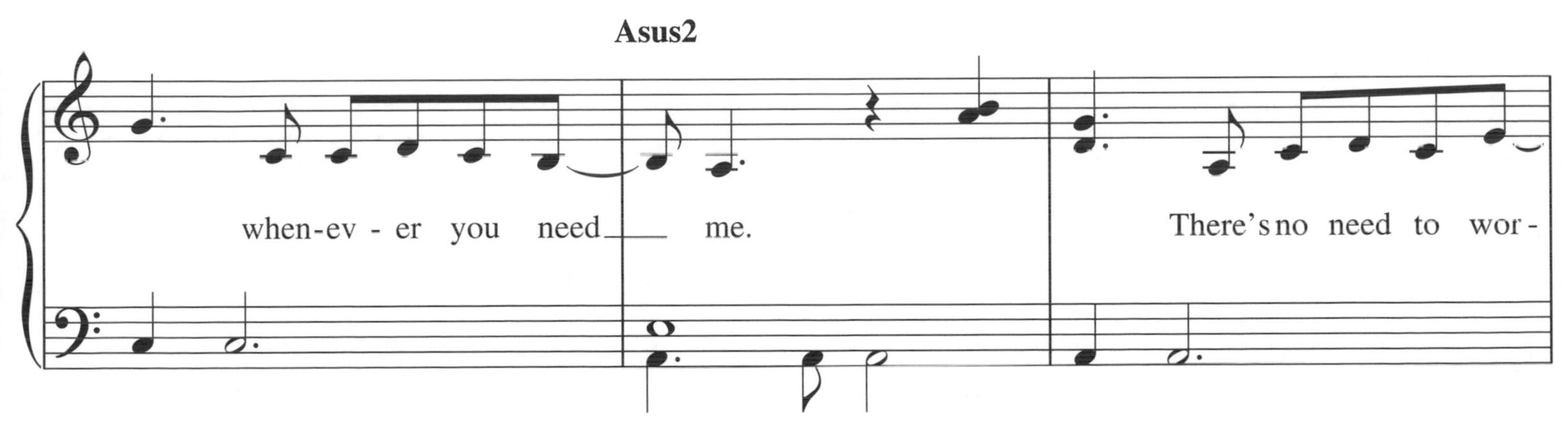
Asus2
when-ev - er you need me.
There's no need to wor -

F
Fmaj7
- ry;
you know that I'm gon - na be

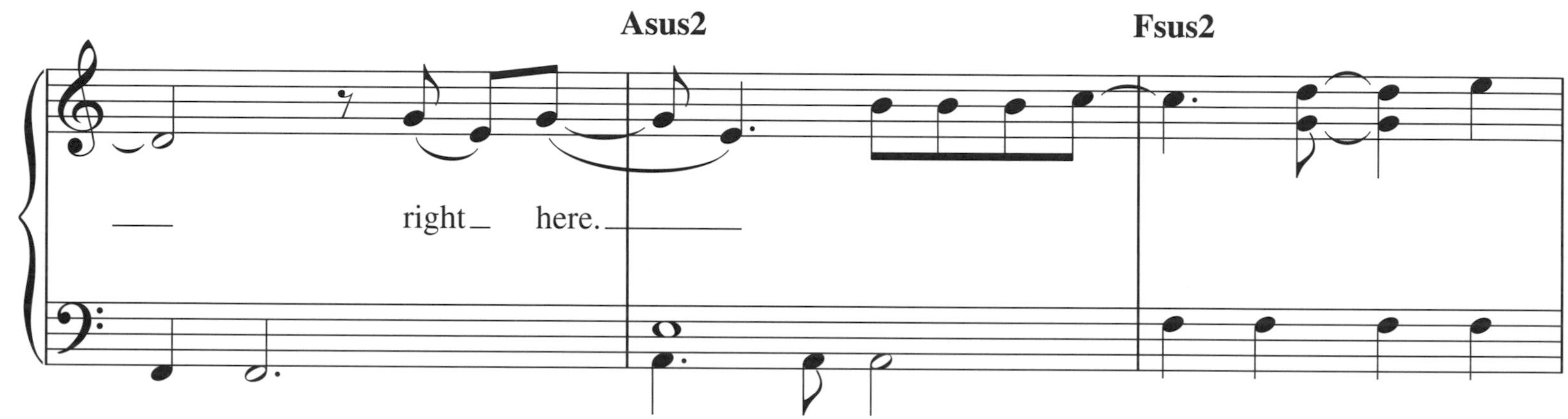
Asus2
Fsus2
right here.

Cmaj7
G5
A5
Ask me once and I'll come,

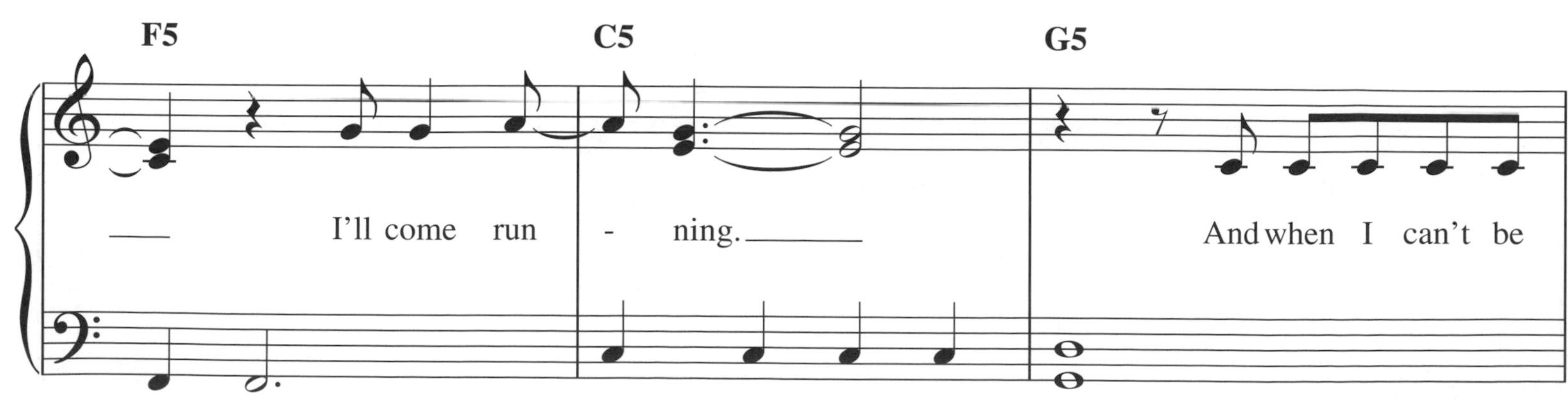
F5
C5
G5
I'll come run - ning.
And when I can't be

Asus2
F5
C
with you, dream me near; keep me in your heart and I'll ap - pear.

G
F5
All you got - ta do is turn a-round, close your eyes, look in - side.

I'm right here.

C5
I'm right here.

CLEAR

Words and Music by DESTINY HOPE CYRUS,
ALEXANDER BARRY and SHELLY PEIKEN

C
F
let it slide.
The
pa - per's not here yet, the
lieve in you.
You
took your chanc - es, and

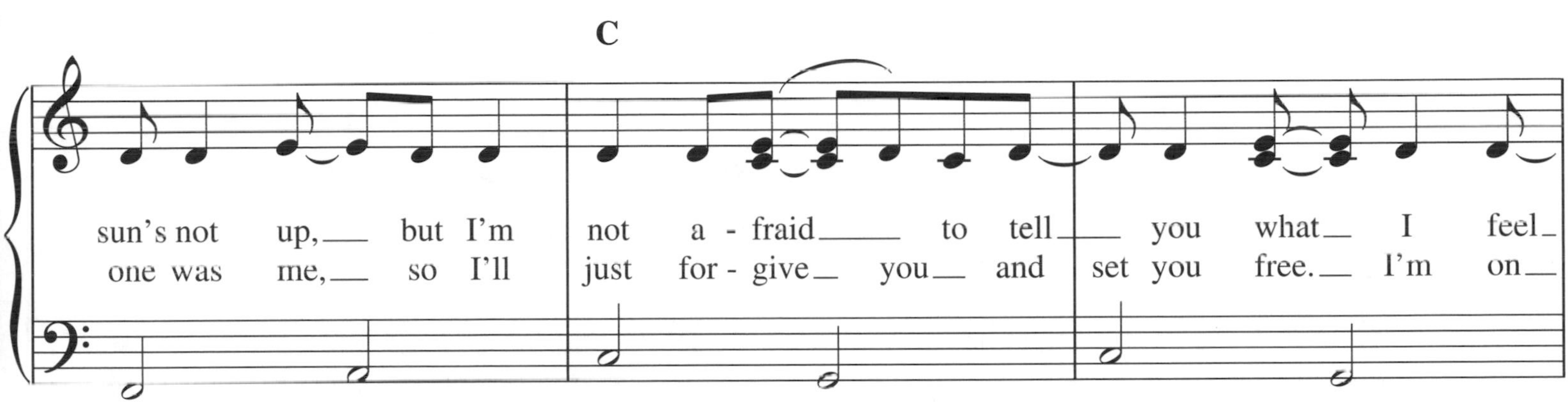
C
sun's not up, but I'm
not a - fraid to tell
you what I feel
one was me, so I'll
just for - give you and
set you free. I'm on

Dm
G
in - side;
I had
one of those dreams that
my way,
yeah, I'm
step - ping out of the

F
C
make it all so
haze, and it's so
clear to me now.
I

Dm
Am
F
got a whole new per - spec - tive. It's so clear to me now, _

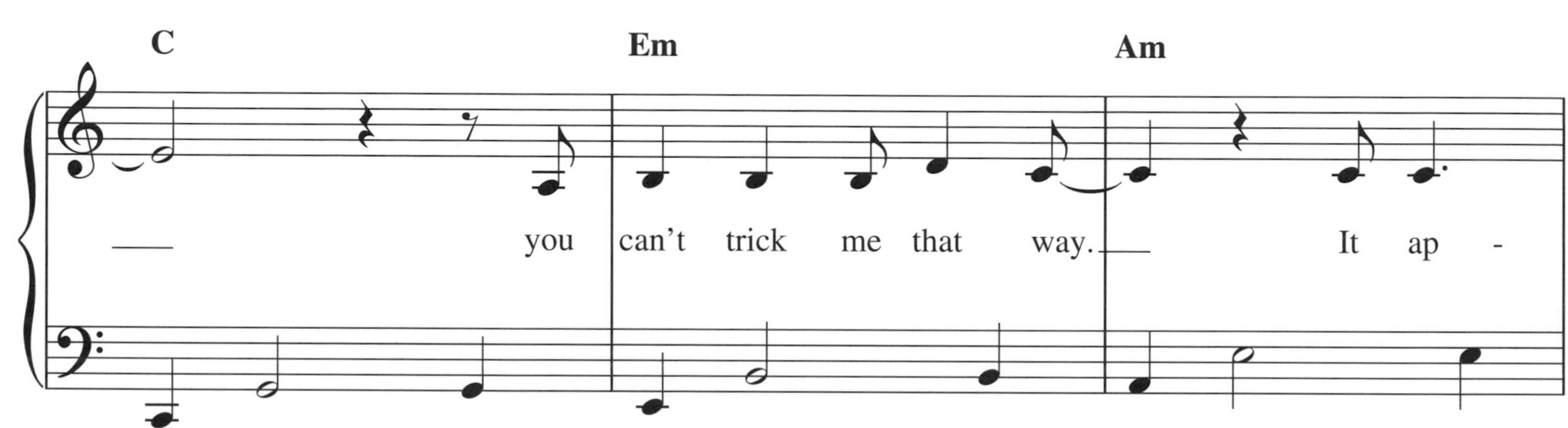
C
Em
Am
_ you can't trick me that way. _ It ap -

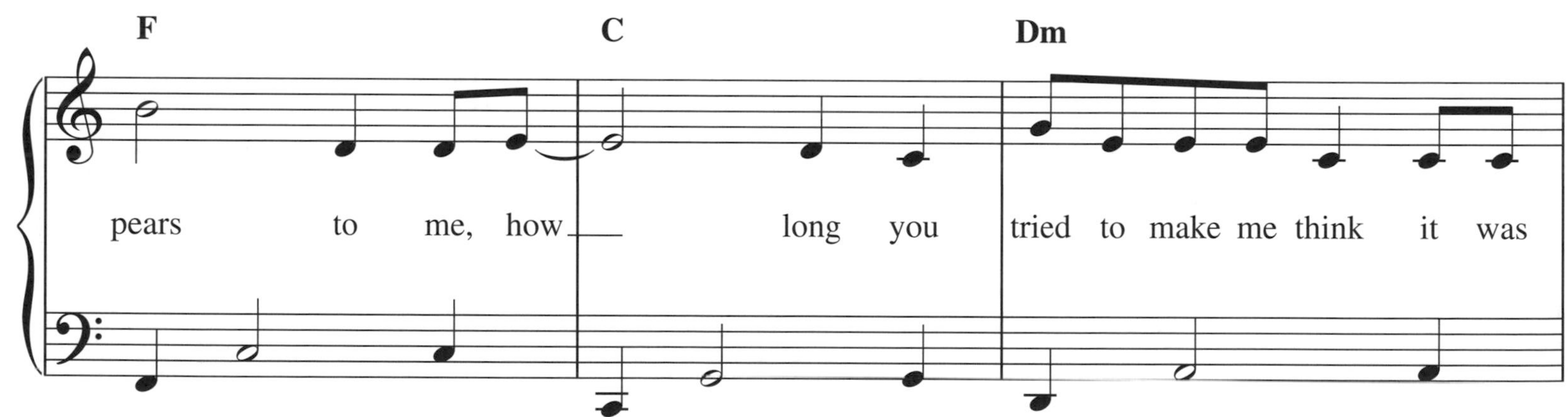
F
C
Dm
pears to me, how _ long you tried to make me think it was

G
To Coda
1.
me, who was be - ing the fake, _ so clear. _

F
C
Dm
G
2.
Am
Why
so clear. I
wan - na put the past be - hind,
Em7
try and may - be I can find
bet - ter days.
The
Am
G
first time in a while, I
think I e - ven feel a smile
on my face.

F
C
I

Dm
Am
F
3
got a whole new per - spec - tive.
Yeah, I do.

C
Em
Am
D.S. al Coda
You can't treat me that way.
It's so

CODA
F
C
so clear.

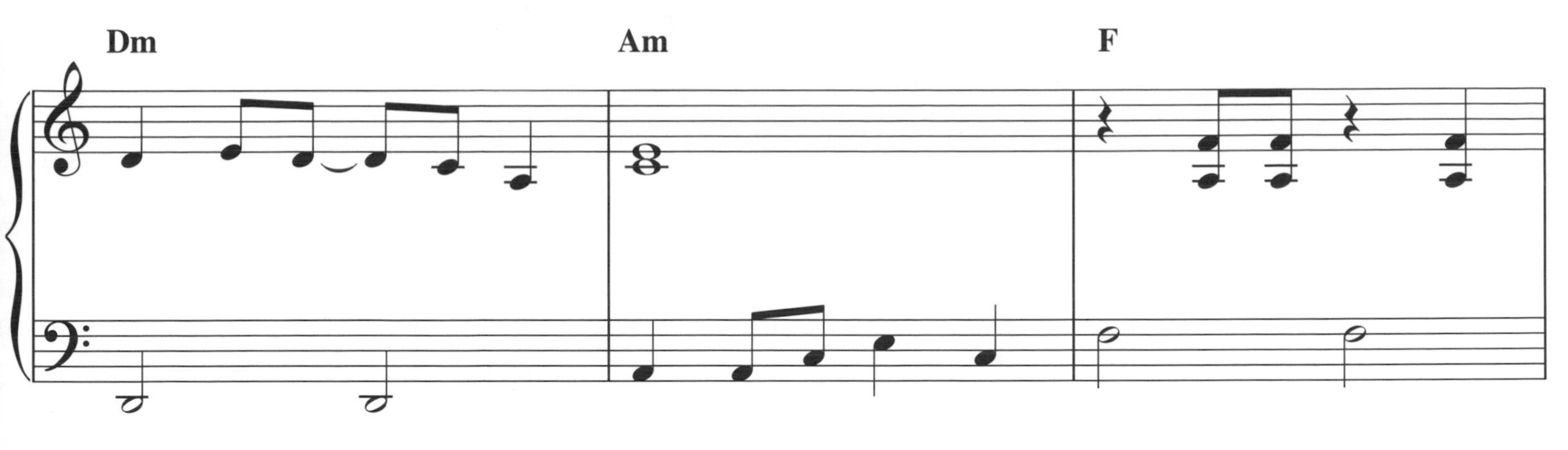
Dm
Am
F

C
Dm
Am
The

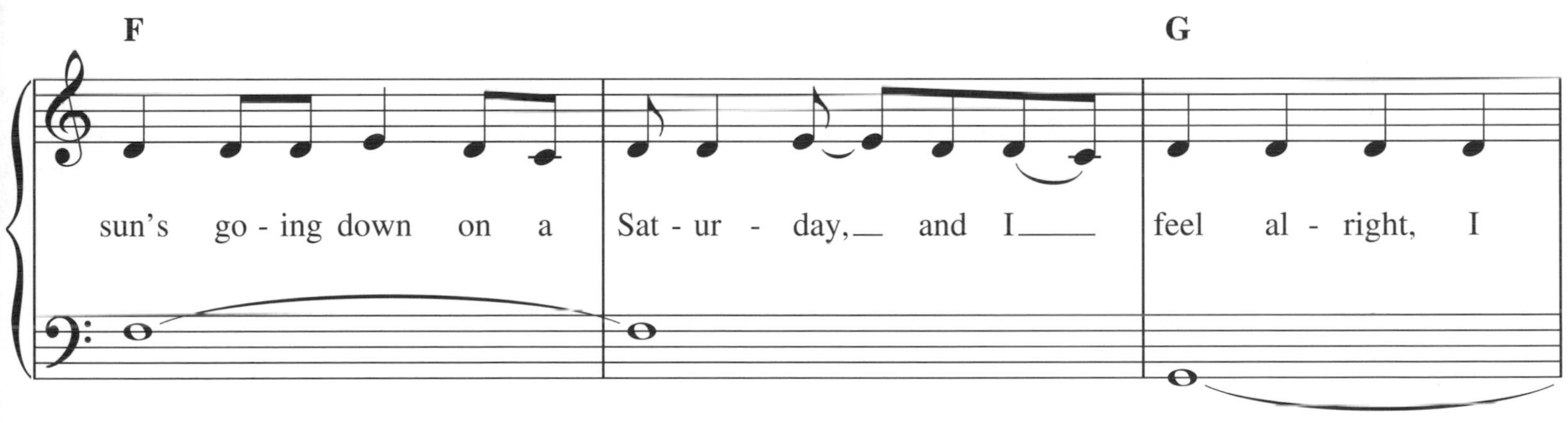
F
G
sun's go - ing down on a Sat - ur - day, and I feel al - right, I

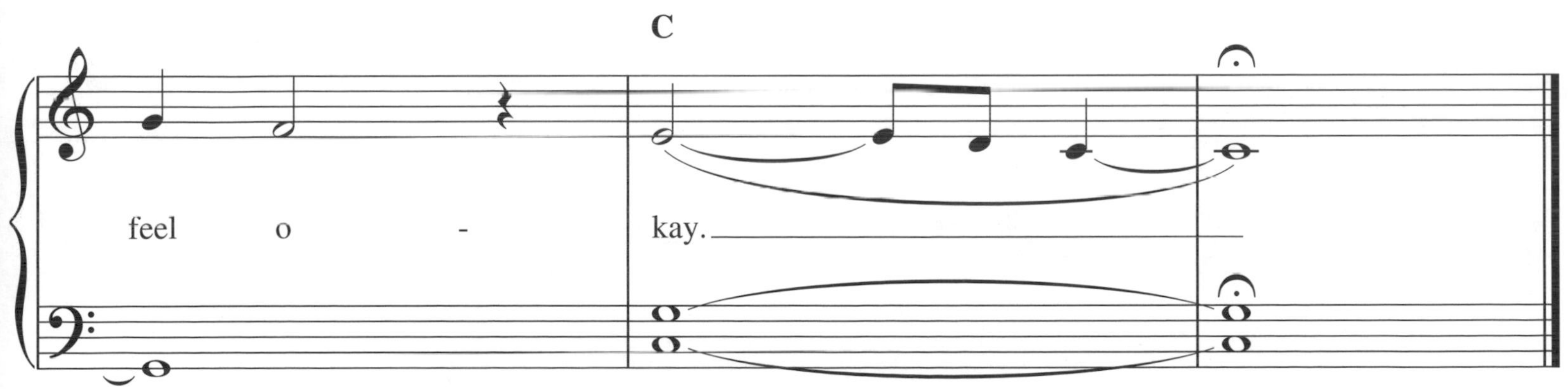
C
feel o - kay.

GOOD AND BROKEN

Words and Music by DESTINY HOPE CYRUS,
TIM JAMES and ANTONINA ARMATO

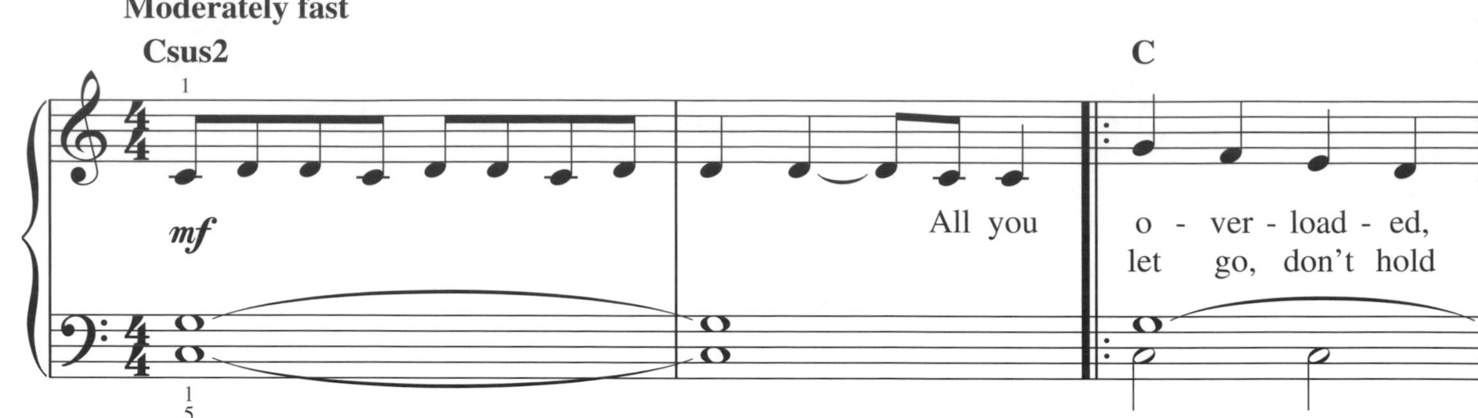

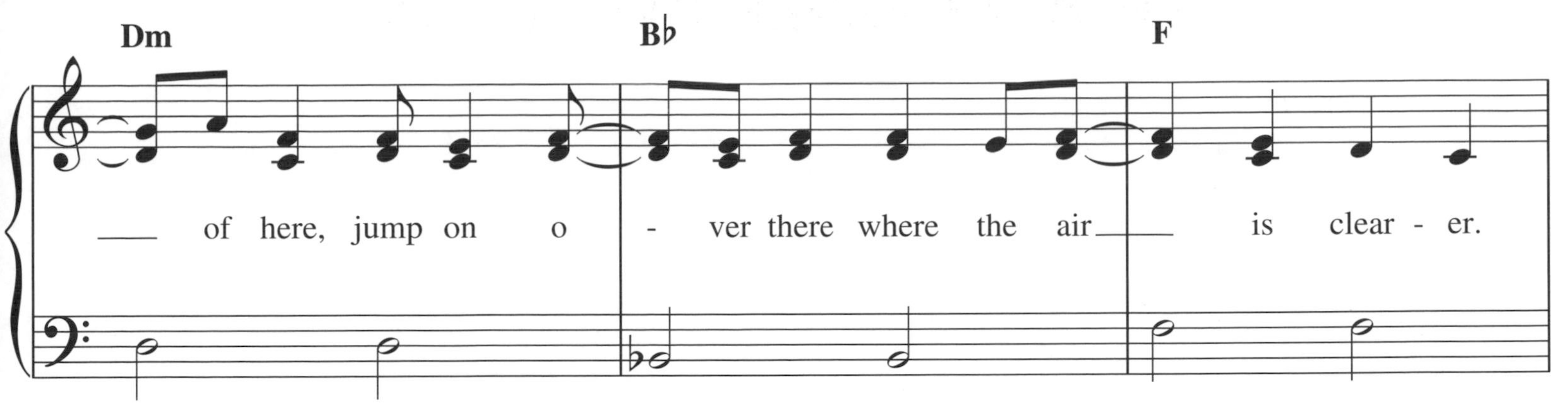

Dm
Bb
F
of here, jump on o - ver there where the air is clear - er.

C
Dm
Bb
We can, we can for - get the pace, win in our own race, be - come

F
C
Dm
a bro - ken chain, yeah. We are bro - ken

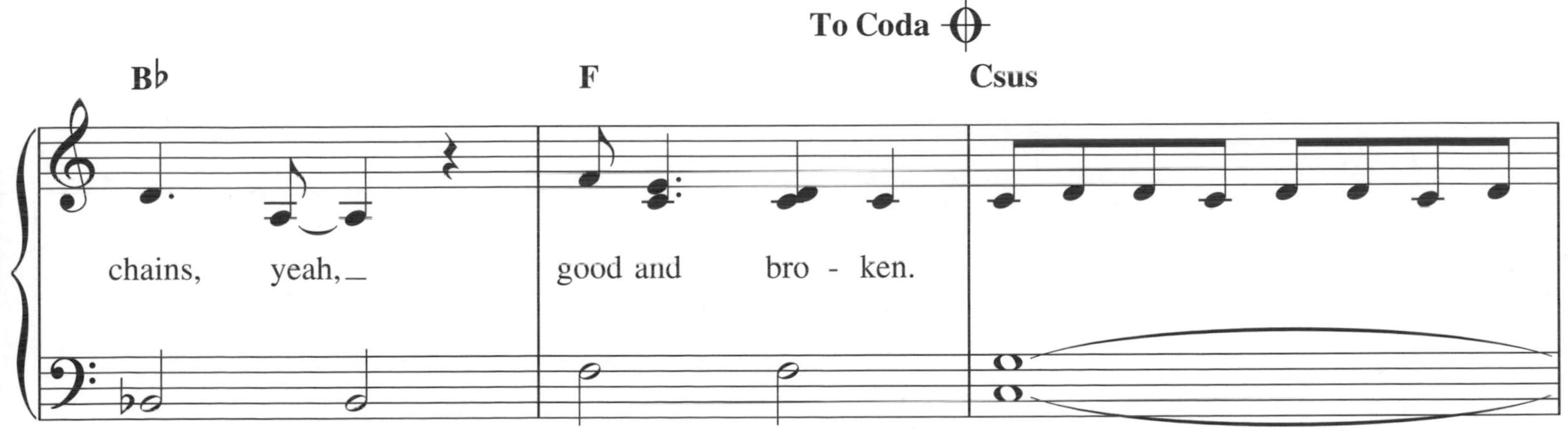

To Coda
Bb
F
Csus
chains, yeah, good and bro - ken.

C
Find the mag - ic, go and grab it; your

D7sus
Csus/B♭
fate is in your hands. Come on, find a rea - son

F
G
D.S. al Coda
to be - lieve in, just tell your - self, "We can."

CODA
C
Dm
B♭

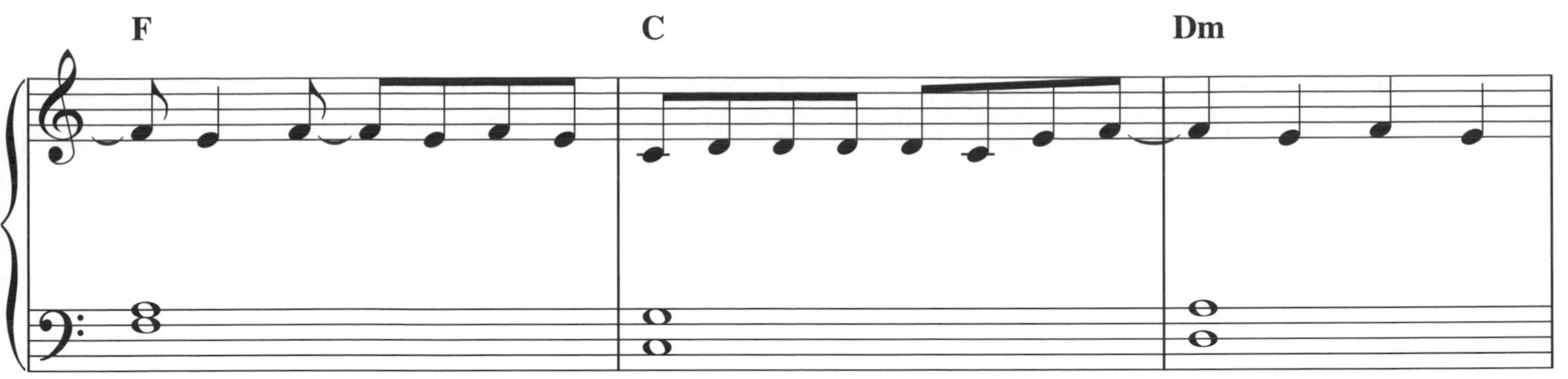
F
C
Dm

B♭
F
C
Get
off your seat, on your feet,

F
Am
G
raise your hands, feel the beat.
Let it go, lose con - trol,
feel it in your soul.

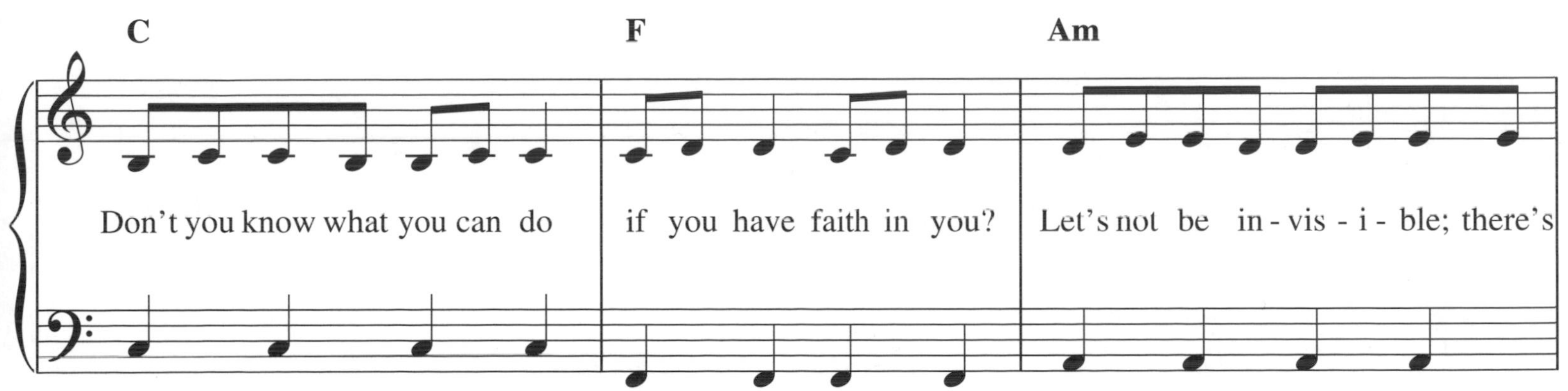
C
F
Am
Don't you know what you can do
if you have faith in you?
Let's not be in - vis - i - ble; there's

G
C
no red light in life; let's go.
We can, we can break out

D
B♭
F
of here, jump on o - ver there where the air is clear - er.

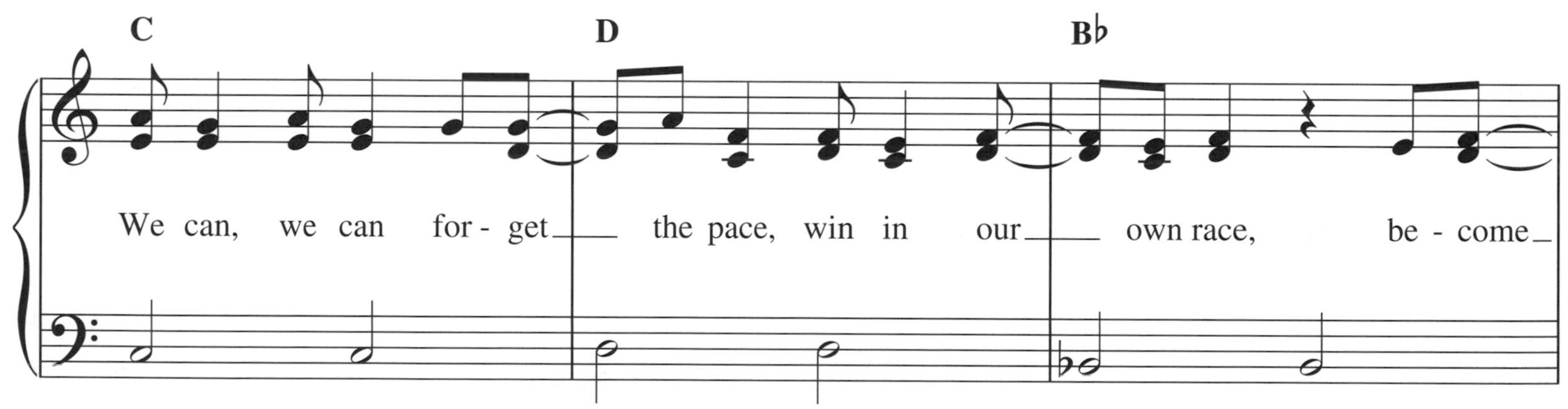
C
D
B♭
We can, we can for - get the pace, win in our own race, be - come

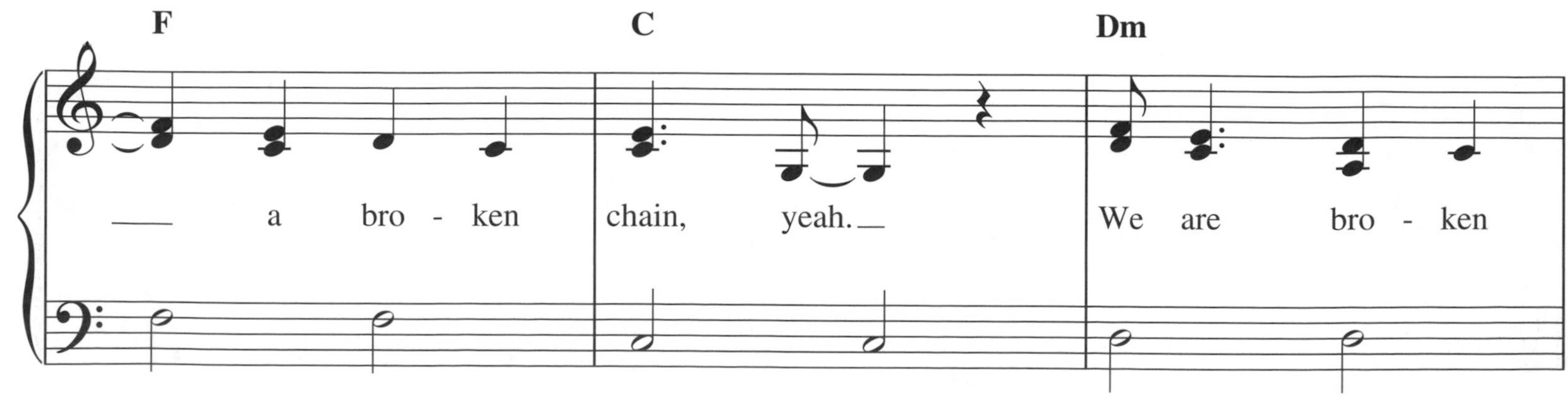
F
C
Dm
a bro - ken chain, yeah.
We are bro - ken

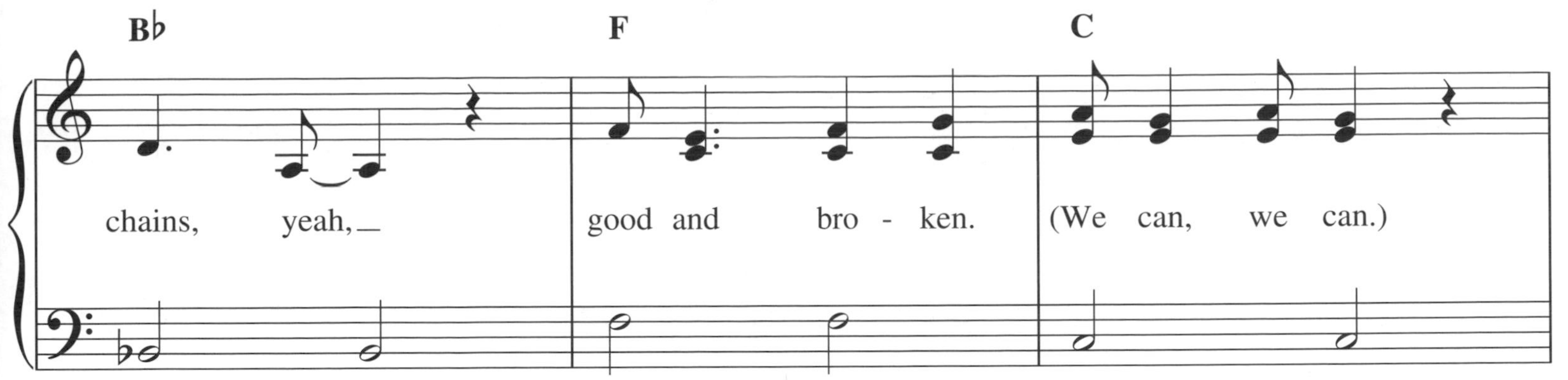
B♭
F
C
chains, yeah,
good and bro - ken.
(We can, we can.)

C/D
B♭
C/F
Oh, we can

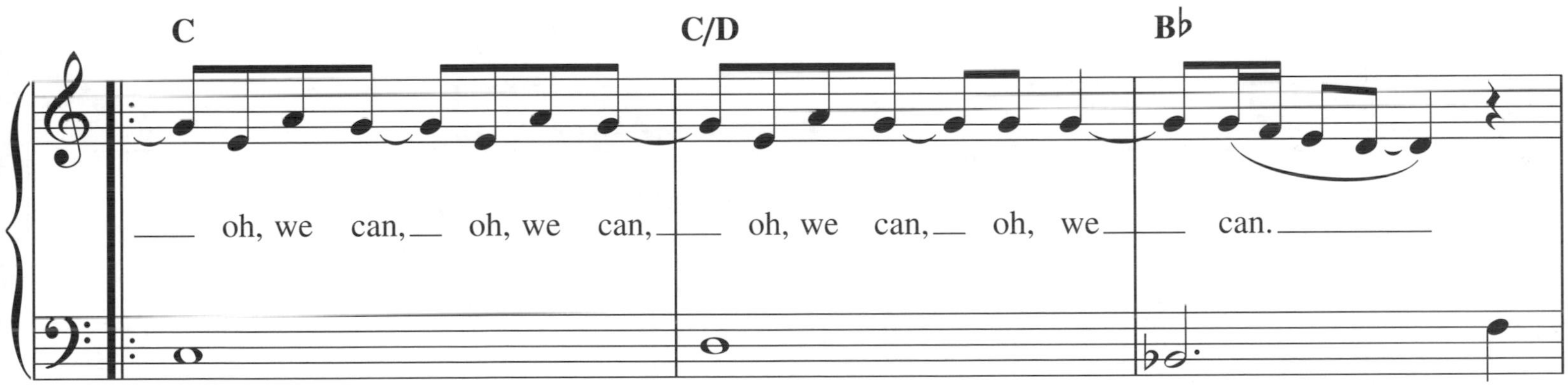
C
C/D
B♭
oh, we can, oh, we can, oh, we can, oh, we can.

1., 2.
3.
F
F
C
Oh, we can,
Good and bro - ken.

I MISS YOU

Words and Music by DESTINY HOPE CYRUS,
BRIAN GREEN and WENDI FOY GREEN

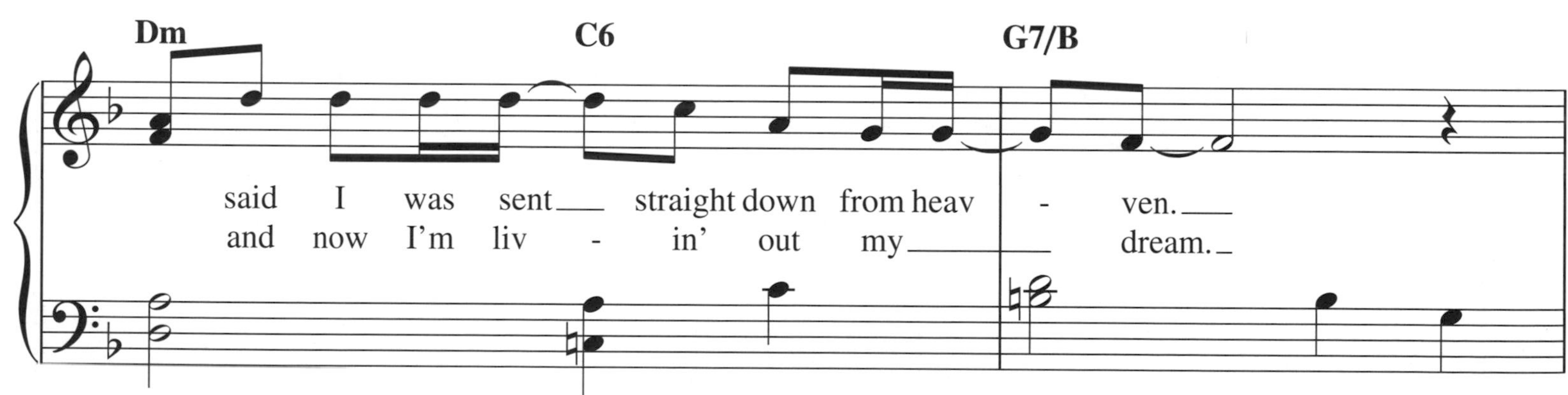

Dm
C6
B♭
loved the way__ you felt so strong.__
ev - 'ry - thing__ that's hap - 'nin' for me.

Gm9
B♭
Csus
C
Dm
I nev - er want - ted you to leave;__ I
I'm think - ing__ back on the past;__ it's

Gm7
B♭
C
want - ed you__ to stay__ here hold - ing me.__
true, the time__ is fly - ing by too__ fast.
I

F
F/E
miss you;__ I miss your smile,_ and

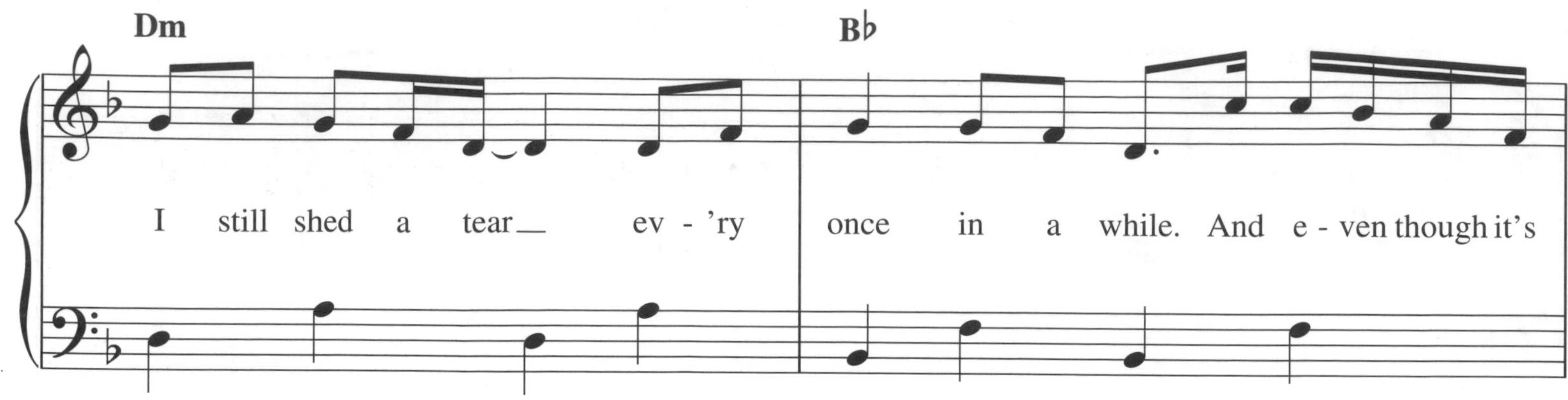
Dm
B♭
I still shed a tear ev - 'ry
once in a while. And e - ven though it's

F
C
C♯m
dif - f'rent now, you're still
here some - how. My

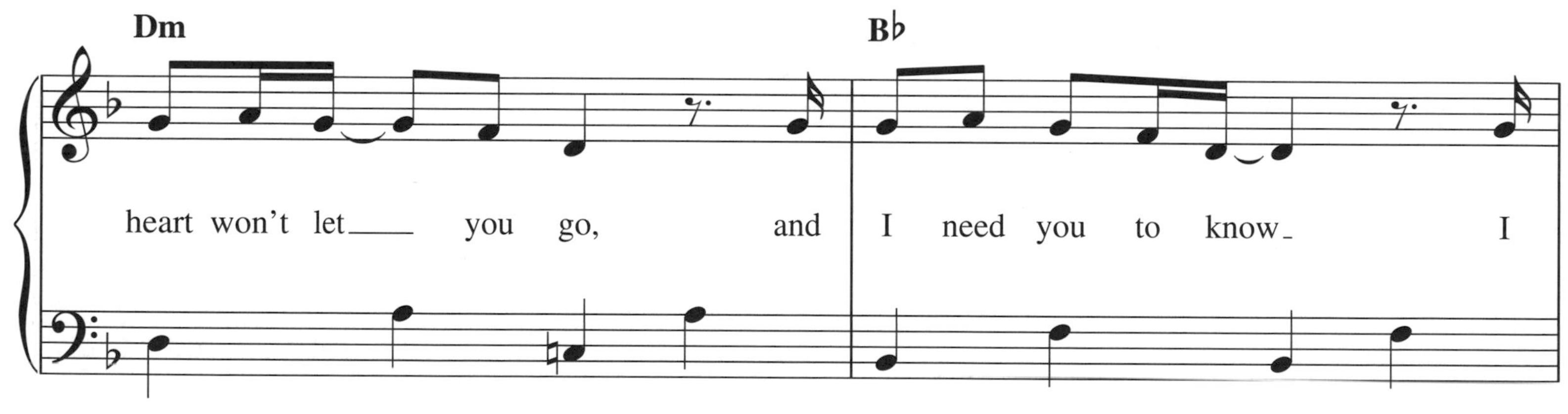
Dm
B♭
heart won't let you go, and
I need you to know I

Gm11
C
miss you.
Sha - la - la - la - la, I

F
B♭/F
Dm7
1.
C
B♭/C
miss you.
2.
C
B♭/C
B♭
I know you're in a bet - ter place, yeah,
C
Dm7
Gm9
F/A
but I wish that I could see your face. Oh,
I know you're where you need to be,
B♭
C/D
D7/F♯
e - ven though it's not here with me.
I

G
G/F♯
miss you; I
miss your smile, and

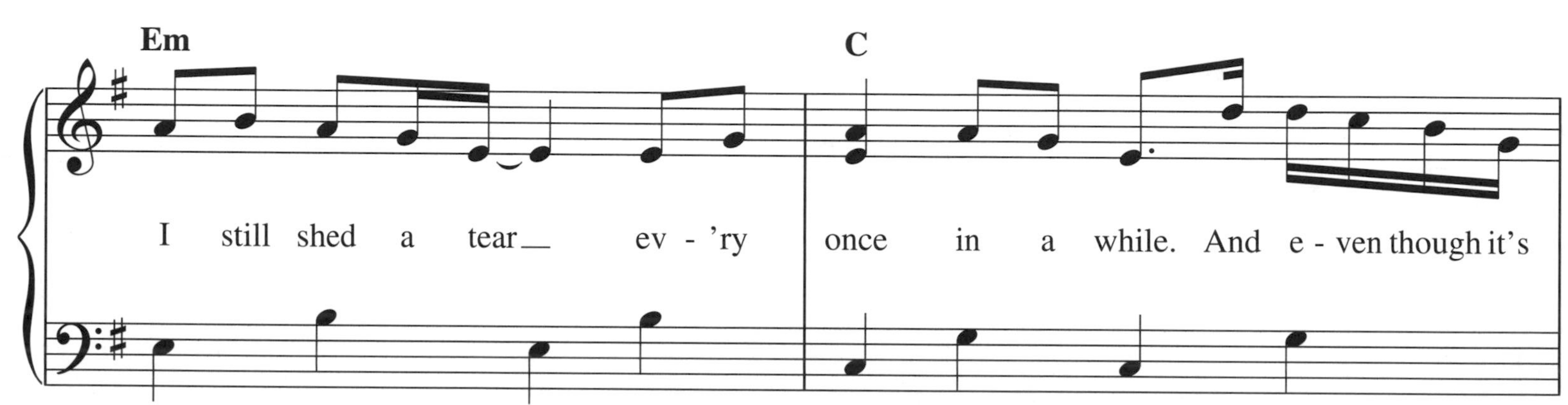
Em
C
I still shed a tear ev - 'ry
once in a while. And e - ven though it's

G
D
D♯m7♭5
dif - f'rent now, you're still
here some - how. My

Em7
G/D
1.
C♯m7♭5
heart won't let you go, and
I need you to know I

Am
D
miss you.
Sha - la - la - la - la,
I

2.
Cmaj7
Am
I need you to know
I
miss you.

D7sus
D
G
Em
Sha - la - la - la - la,
I
miss you.

D
C
G